Synonyms and Antonyms Vocabulary and Cloze

The 1000 Word 11+ Brain Boost

Part

2

The Eureka! 11+ Confidence series

CEM-style Practice Exam Papers covering:
Comprehension, Verbal Reasoning,
Non-Verbal Reasoning and Numerical Reasoning

Numerical Reasoning: Advanced Training Workbooks

Tough exam paper questions and detailed explanations of how to tackle them, to increase speed and reduce error.

Verbal Reasoning: Advanced Training Workbooks

The *1000-Word Brain Boost* is a powerful, intensive course teaching Synonyms, Antonyms, Odd-One-Out, Analogy, Vocabulary and Cloze in CEM-style questions. Its famous *Explanations* section explains hundreds of language subtleties and distinctions that many 11+ candidates find challenging.

Non-Verbal Reasoning: The *Non-Verbal Ninja* Training Course

The *Non-Verbal Ninja* is an intensive *visual* course for core CEM exam skills. The 3 training workbooks include over 600 puzzles coupled with *visual* explanations. They build both fundamental skills and the crucial confidence to seek out rules without having to have them explained first. Each book rapidly moves on from simple levels to challenging training puzzles that enhance the capacities of even the strongest 11+ hopefuls.

Please check the website **www.eureka11plus.org/updates** for updates and clarifications to this book.

Publication date 7 August 2015

First Published in the United Kingdom by
Eureka! Eleven Plus Exams **www.eureka11plus.org** Email: **office@eureka11plus.org**

Eureka! Eleven Plus Exams expresses its gratitude to Mr Dan Thomson.

ISBN-13: 978-1515250081
ISBN-10: 1515250083

We are all human and vulnerable to error. Eureka! Eleven Plus is very grateful to any reader who notifies us on office@eureka11plus.org of an unnoticed error, so we can immediately correct it and provide a tangible reward.

Helping your child prepare for 11+ Verbal Reasoning questions

Verbal Reasoning is a cornerstone of the 11+ examination. It is intended to test familiarity with vocabulary, grammar and usage of words. The best grounding for this section of the exam is a broad and voracious interest in reading, which brings the pupil into frequent contact with a substantial spectrum of vocabulary.

In the run-up to the 11+ examination, however, the limited time is best targeted on challenging words and experience of the layout of the actual 11+ examination.

The 1000 Word Brain Boost is a series of two books, each containing over 500 CEM-style practice exam paper questions, structured into short minute training sessions, and providing answers and explanations. It delivers:

- An intense **learning workout** on words that many pupils may find difficult
- Questions laid out in modern format resembling exam papers to build familiarity
- A thorough spectrum of question types including
    - Synonyms
    - Antonyms
    - Words that do not match a specified word
    - Odd one out
    - Analogy (Similar relationships)
    - Spelling (Find the missing letters)
    - Cloze (Find the missing word)
- An answer section giving explanations including a word definition.

This intense training scheme, applied in short bursts over many days, will focus the pupil's attention on a thousand words that can prove difficult at 11+ level. To obtain the maximum benefit, please encourage your child to fill in the section at the end of each session:

- They should *list* the words they found unfamiliar.
- They should *write* a short sentence using each word.

It is important to explain to the pupil that these books form a **learning resource**, concentrating on *hard* words in the vocabulary that can come up this level. They should expect to find many unfamiliar words in each training session, and recognise this as a learning opportunity. The real 11+ exam will contain many much simpler questions: they do not appear in this intense training course.

- It is theoretically ideal to carry out the training sessions formally: pupil seated alone, away from any distractions. However, some children enjoy doing one session at a time during car journeys; seize any opportunity to exploit their enthusiasm.
- Immediately after the session, encourage the pupil to mark their own work. Immediacy and involvement increase interest – and perhaps even enjoyment – in exam preparation.
- Insist on discussing the questions which were not answered correctly. Reassure your child that the Brain Boost focuses on more difficult words, so contains fewer easy questions than the real exam. The purpose of this training system is not to predict their exam mark but to increase it.
- Most importantly, join with your child in *using* each of their own personal "unfamiliar words" in the day's conversation. Introduce discussion of otherwise-unnecessary subjects to provide an opportunity for this. This may feel incongruous, but it is better to have laughter at this stage than later bemusement in a lonely 11+ examination hall.

Once they have finished the 1000 Word Brain Boost, ask them to collate their self-written tables of difficult words from the ends of each test into a single resource. This process is valuable revision. In the final run-up to the exam you can focus on this list with them, gradually striking off words as they become familiar with them.

To see Verbal Reasoning questions in the context of other question types, we suggest the *Eureka! 11+ Confidence* series of multiple-choice exam papers:

- Question papers with the modern multiple-choice format used by CEM and others.
- Answer sheets laid out in modern format (in places requiring digit-by-digit entry)
- Full answers with explanations
- Supplementary books giving detailed methods, tips and tricks on the more challenging aspects of Numerical Reasoning

Thoughtful support from parents can be crucial for pupils in the run-up to examinations. Use the 1000 Word Brain Boost, the Eureka! Practice Exam Papers and Numerical Reasoning advanced training workbooks to help them reach their full potential.

Using the 1000-Word Brain Boost to advance your Verbal Reasoning skills

Doing the training sessions

If you can, find a place where you will be undisturbed for 10-15 minutes. Ensure the background is quiet: no TV, radio, computer, music or chat. Your adults may want to help but ask them to do this at the end of each session, not during it. Make your marks in the manner required in the exam. Below is an example.

Right
Right
Wrong
Wrong
Wrong

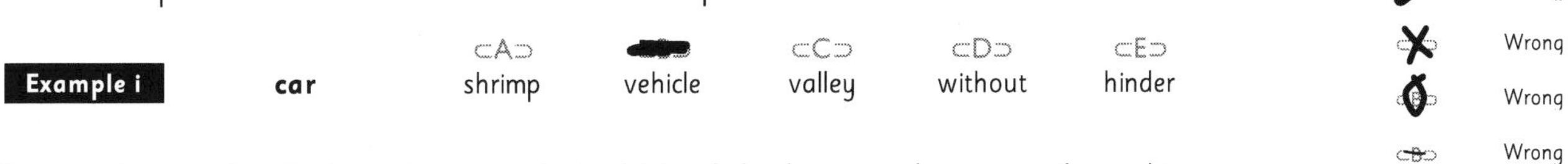

The mark must be dark and run the full width of the box, as shown on the right.

Unsure what a word means?

Congratulations! This is an opportunity to learn. Decide which options are clearly wrong. In the real exam you should then choose the most plausible of the remaining options (since no answer guarantees no mark). During the Brain Boost, however, you do not need to guess. Just cross out the clearly wrong options as this is part of the training, and wait to read the explanation afterwards.

Learn from the explanations at the back

The Brain Boosting really begins immediately after the answering process. Read the explanations at the back. This is more important than checking whether your answer was right, because it increases your knowledge.

Brain Boost questions are deliberately tough

The Brain Boost intentionally teaches words that pupils at your stage find difficult. In the real exam and other preparation books there will be many more familiar words, but practicing words you already find easy does not boost your brain.

Build your personal library

At the end of each training session, write down the ***question*** words or ***correct option*** words you found unfamiliar or problematic.

For each word, make up your own sentence using it, as shown in the example below.

Word	A short sentence *you* have created, using the word
surpassed	*After the Brain Boost, my confidence in vocabulary surpassed even my boldest hopes.*

Consolidate using your adults

Where you did not get the right answer, discuss the explanatory text with your adults. Do not be embarrassed: even adults will find some of these skill-stretching questions difficult.

Explain to your adults that you want to practice using these unfamiliar words. Build them into your conversation. This may require talking about strange things. Your adults really want you to perform at your best in the exam and will likely be happy to assist. It might even be fun!

Final revision

Nearer the exam, collate your lists of unfamiliar words from all the Brain Boost sessions. Delete the ones you have now learnt to use and produce a master list of still-unfamiliar words. Continue to work on using those words in conversation, deleting them as they become familiar.

Training Session 18

Matching Words

Identify which word is MOST SIMILAR in meaning to the word on the left. Each question has only one best answer. For each question shade your one chosen answer.

		A	B	C	D	E
1	**serendipity**	relaxing	coincidence	termination	submerging	misery
2	**route**	destroy	pathway	departure	exit	timely
3	**rant**	tirade	reply	trouser	managed	insect
4	**quench**	smell	extinguish	uncertainty	tighten	peculiar
5	**proximity**	error	roundness	closeness	airflow	rigidity
6	**protocol**	remnant	trial	procedure	original	spinner
7	**amuse**	cheer	dislocate	baffle	discover	educate

Opposite Words

Identify which word is MOST OPPOSITE in meaning to the word on the left. Each question has only one best answer. For each question shade your one chosen answer.

		A	B	C	D	E
8	**evanescent**	steamy	arid	noiseless	solid	permanent
9	**dazzling**	immemorial	unmemorable	inveterate	indiscernible	drizzling

Words That Do Not Match

Identify which of the 5 options A-E matches LEAST WELL in meaning to the word on the left. There is only one best answer. Shade your one chosen answer.

		A	B	C	D	E
10	**schedule**	listing	plan	programme	occasion	organize
11	**content**	subject	appease	anger	matter	satisfy

Odd One Out

Each group has four words which can have similar meanings, and one word which is different. Find the odd one out. Shade your one chosen answer.

	A	B	C	D	E
12	pure	immaculate	blameless	waterproof	spotless
13	careless	superficial	negligent	open-minded	uninterested

Go to the next page 

14

A	B	C	D	E
mournful	doleful	melancholy	night-time	gloomy

15

A	B	C	D	E
unreal	misleading	elusive	deceptive	illusive

16

A	B	C	D	E
soberly	sedately	gravelly	seriously	solemnly

17

A	B	C	D	E
intimate	confident	friend	confidant	adviser

Find The Missing Letters

Complete the sentence by identifying the missing letters. Write one letter into each of the large boxes below. After writing each letter, shade its corresponding element in the A-Z block beside it.

18 I realise the hotel is full and it is late in the evening, but my wife is heavily pregnant and we are a long way away from any other hotels. Please could you try hard to see if you can acco□□□□ate us?

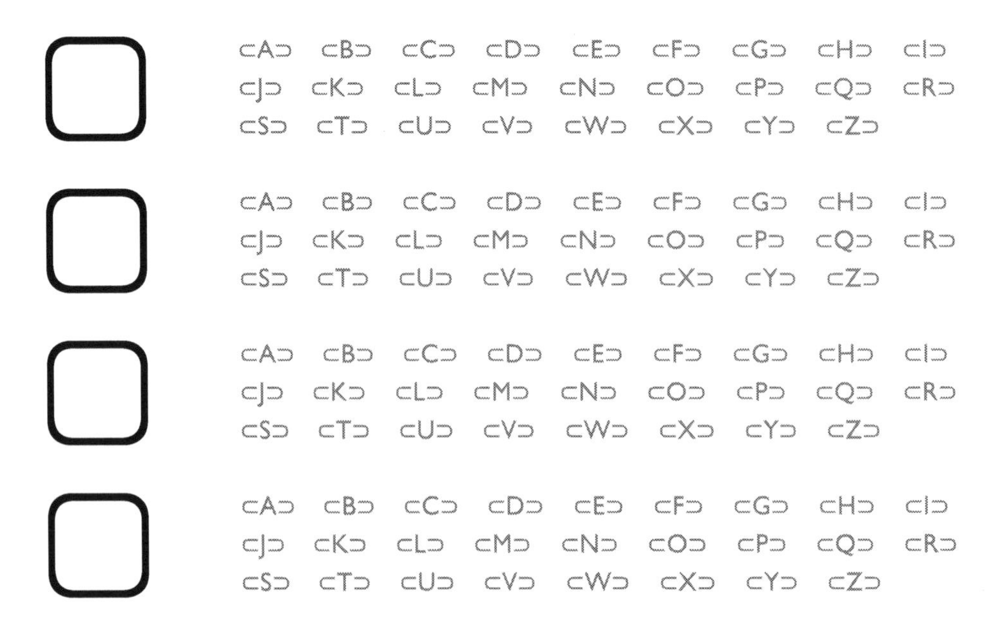

Similar relationships

Each sentence below states that one relationship is similar to another relationship. Choose the word, from options A to E, that completes the sentence best.

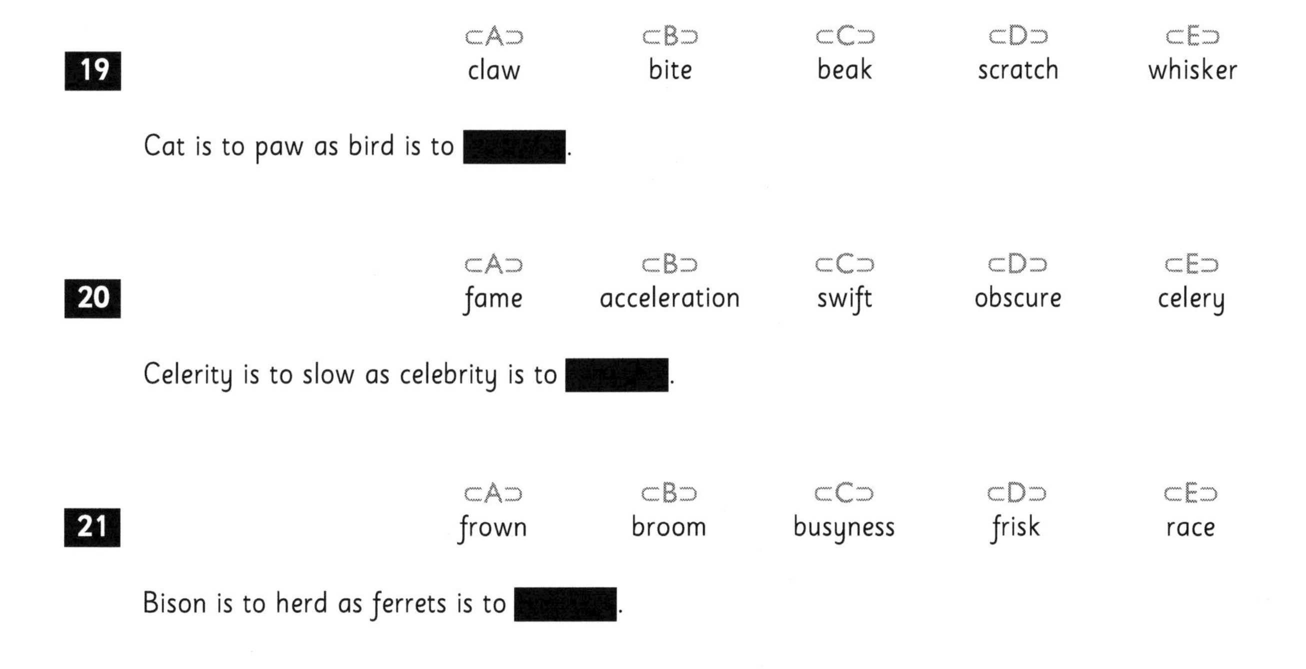

19

A	B	C	D	E
claw	bite	beak	scratch	whisker

Cat is to paw as bird is to ______.

20

A	B	C	D	E
fame	acceleration	swift	obscure	celery

Celerity is to slow as celebrity is to ______.

21

A	B	C	D	E
frown	broom	busyness	frisk	race

Bison is to herd as ferrets is to ______.

Find The Missing Word

In each of the following pieces of text, one word is missing.
Complete it by choosing the one option A to E which fits best.

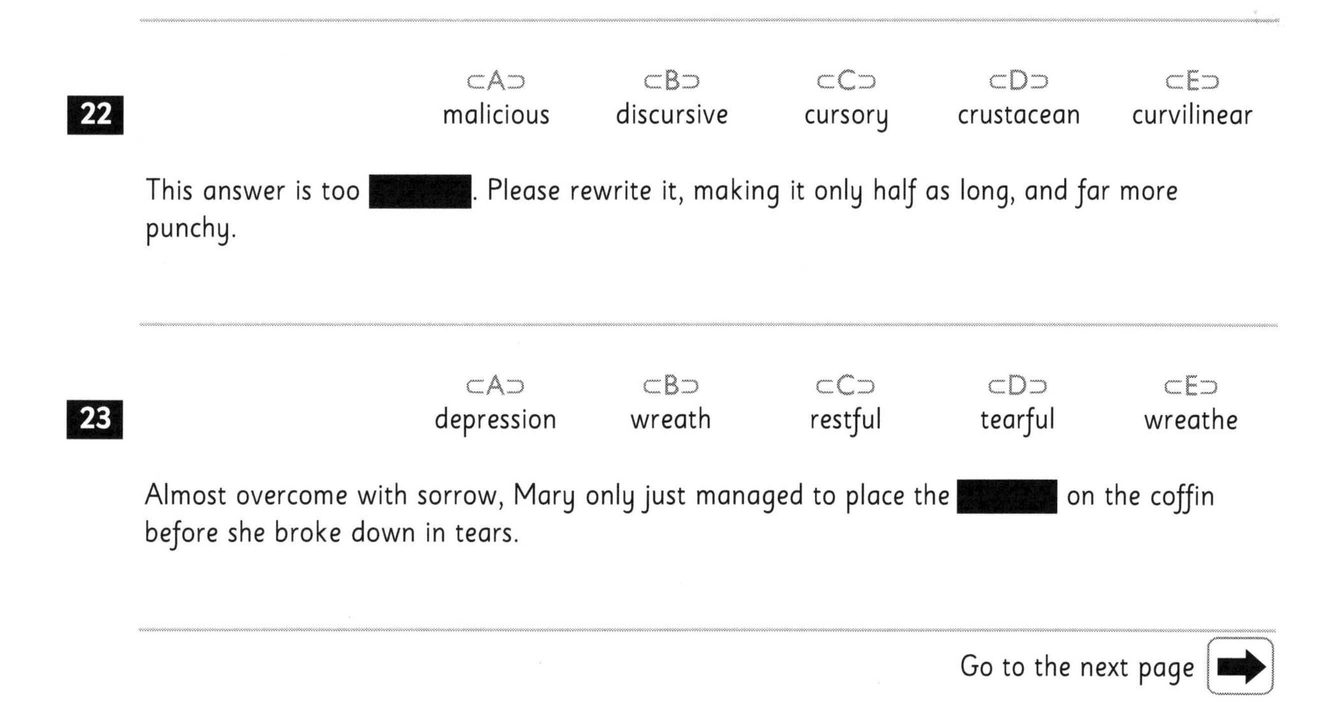

22

A	B	C	D	E
malicious	discursive	cursory	crustacean	curvilinear

This answer is too ______. Please rewrite it, making it only half as long, and far more punchy.

23

A	B	C	D	E
depression	wreath	restful	tearful	wreathe

Almost overcome with sorrow, Mary only just managed to place the ______ on the coffin before she broke down in tears.

Go to the next page ➡

24

⊂A⊃	⊂B⊃	⊂C⊃	⊂D⊃	⊂E⊃
accept	deviate	except	derive	extinguish

Whatever the excuse you provide, the rule is firm and I cannot _______ you from it.

25

⊂A⊃	⊂B⊃	⊂C⊃	⊂D⊃	⊂E⊃
discordant	revelatory	intercollegiate	orienteered	replicative

Your goals for this meeting are _______ with ours, because we have almost completely different motivations.

26

⊂A⊃	⊂B⊃	⊂C⊃	⊂D⊃	⊂E⊃
queue	sly	cue	slay	slew

Now seeing the full enormity of the _______ that had developed, she regretted not having joined it at the earliest opportunity.

27

⊂A⊃	⊂B⊃	⊂C⊃	⊂D⊃	⊂E⊃
approximate	practise	approval	practice	proxy

The dreadful din emerging from next door turned out to be piano _______. We only gained respite when the poor child's mother, driven to distraction, shooed him out into the sun to play.

28

⊂A⊃	⊂B⊃	⊂C⊃	⊂D⊃	⊂E⊃
turban	turbid	turret	turmeric	turgid

He was happy to read and comment on a short note, but totally flummoxed to be presented with ten thousand words of _______ prose.

29

A	B	C	D	E
dessert	desert	deserve	deserted	deserved

Viewed from a satellite, the broad expanse of ______ was studded with green dots which were oases.

30

A	B	C	D	E
arrange	find	erode	wear	levitate

It took millions of years for the river to gradually ______ the great canyon we see now, through the effect of untold millions of pebbles and billions of gallons of water.

This is the end of the training session.

Read the explanations at the back. In the box below, note any words you came across that were unfamiliar, together with a meaning or an example of usage. Practice using these words with adults.

Word	A short sentence *you* have created, using the word

Training Session 19

Matching Words

Identify which word is MOST SIMILAR in meaning to the word on the left. Each question has only one best answer. For each question shade your one chosen answer.

		A	B	C	D	E
1	**proliferation**	opposition	anti-abortion	growth	verbosity	rejuvenation
2	**pivotal**	election	revolving	desperate	crucial	twisted
3	**pervasive**	horrible	convincing	intruding	clever	rife
4	**omen**	cinema	okay	domestic	warning	female
5	**recite**	narrate	withdraw	relocate	answer	document
6	**fertile**	secretive	roofing	thirtieth	slate	productive
7	**contrived**	restarted	genuine	artificial	attempted	deducted

Opposite Words

Identify which word is MOST OPPOSITE in meaning to the word on the left. Each question has only one best answer. For each question shade your one chosen answer.

		A	B	C	D	E
8	**fleeting**	momentary	massive	permanent	momentous	accumulating
9	**euphoria**	depression	dispersal	confidence	boost	challenge

Words That Do Not Match

Identify which of the 5 options A-E matches LEAST WELL in meaning to the word on the left. There is only one best answer. Shade your one chosen answer.

		A	B	C	D	E
10	**virtue**	goodness	strength	morality	purity	nobleness
11	**counterfeit**	answer	fake	imitation	phony	reproduce

Odd One Out

Each group has four words which can have similar meanings, and one word which is different. Find the odd one out. Shade your one chosen answer.

	A	B	C	D	E
12	wide	vast	broad	extensive	specious
13	believable	pulsatile	plausible	deceptive	misleading

Go to the next page ➡

14 (A) expose (B) discover (C) divulge (D) reveal (E) disclose

15 (A) treaty (B) shrink (C) contract (D) agreement (E) convention

16 (A) bother (B) perspex (C) vex (D) confound (E) perplex

17 (A) stick (B) match (C) tally (D) correspond (E) agree

Find The Missing Letters

Complete the sentence by identifying the missing letters. Write one letter into each of the large boxes below. After writing each letter, shade its corresponding element in the A-Z block beside it.

18 As the act drew to its climax, the au□□□□ce were on the edge of their seats, eyes fixed upon the young woman's hands and feet still wriggling as the giant saw plunged through the flimsy box in which she lay.

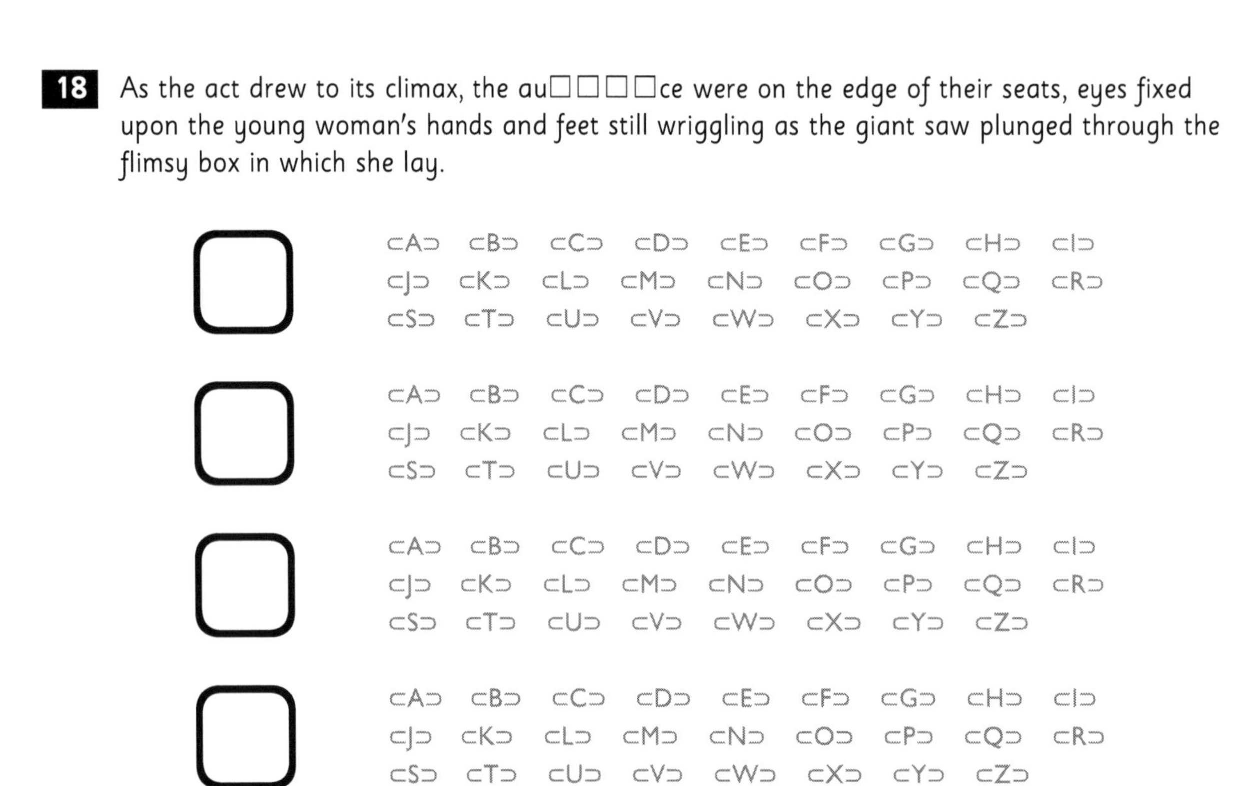

Similar relationships

Each sentence below states that one relationship is similar to another relationship. Choose the word, from options A to E, that completes the sentence best.

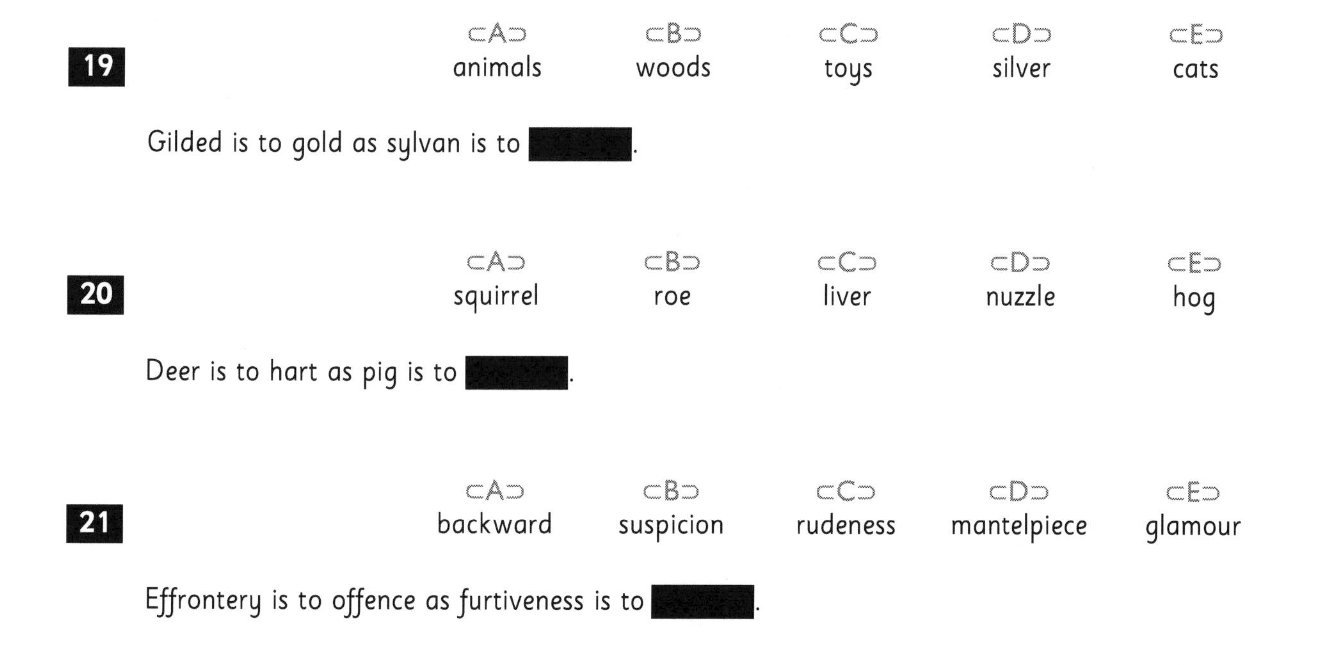

19

A	B	C	D	E
animals	woods	toys	silver	cats

Gilded is to gold as sylvan is to ______.

20

A	B	C	D	E
squirrel	roe	liver	nuzzle	hog

Deer is to hart as pig is to ______.

21

A	B	C	D	E
backward	suspicion	rudeness	mantelpiece	glamour

Effrontery is to offence as furtiveness is to ______.

Find The Missing Word

In each of the following pieces of text, one word is missing.
Complete it by choosing the one option A to E which fits best.

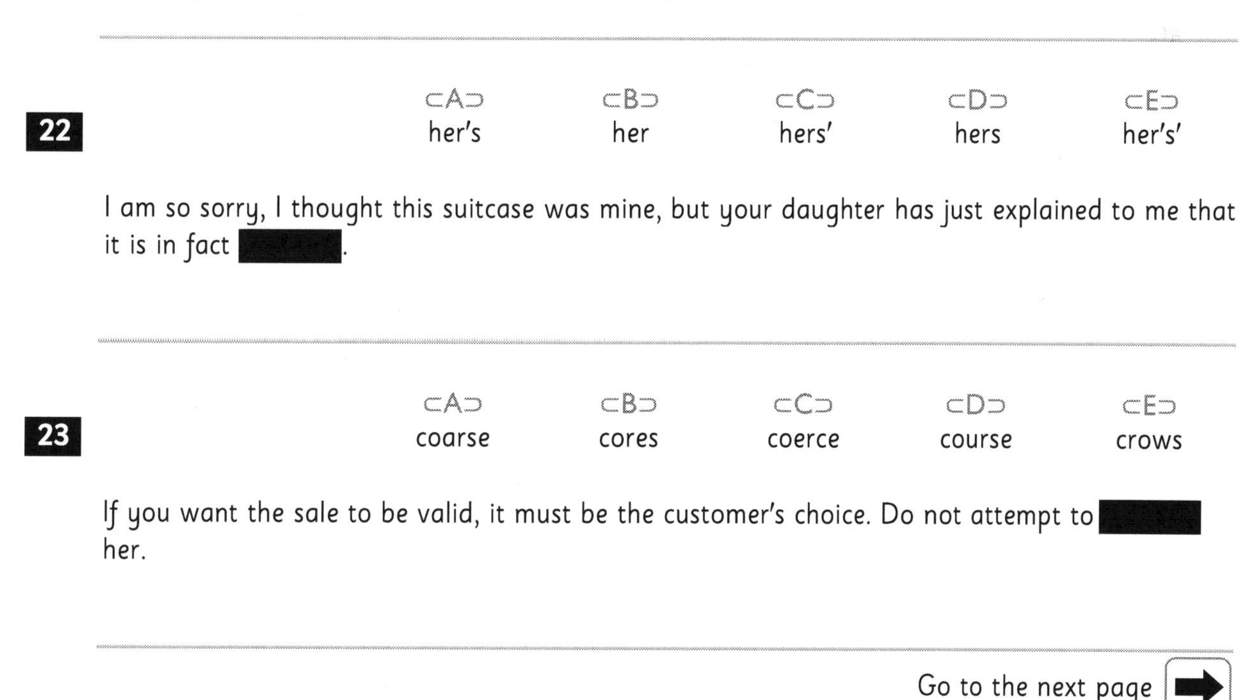

22

A	B	C	D	E
her's	her	hers'	hers	her's'

I am so sorry, I thought this suitcase was mine, but your daughter has just explained to me that it is in fact ______.

23

A	B	C	D	E
coarse	cores	coerce	course	crows

If you want the sale to be valid, it must be the customer's choice. Do not attempt to ______ her.

Go to the next page

24

A	B	C	D	E
affect	afflict	effect	inflict	infect

Suffering from the limp I have borne since childhood, I was a sitting duck as he raised his club to ______ the final shattering blow.

25

A	B	C	D	E
cue	show	queue	chew	crew

Just on ______, Sylvia leapt onto the stage in her angel costume, causing gasps of amazement from the audience.

26

A	B	C	D	E
temptation	overflowing	rudimentary	incomparable	despicable

It was ______ of the company to proceed with the dam building that flooded those thousands of homes without making provision for the displaced people to be suitably rehoused.

27

A	B	C	D	E
expect	accept	axe	except	aspect

With the wind gusting so sharply, I ______ this evening to see a fair number of trees blown over.

28

A	B	C	D	E
bonnet	cupboard	windscreen	vehicle	radio

Hearing a clanking sound in the engine, he pulled up in a lay-by and opened the ______.

29

(A)	(B)	(C)	(D)	(E)
disperse	stealth	roar	chase	predator

The arrival of the lioness saw the entire heard of gazelle ▬▬▬ in a flurry of hooves and horns.

30

(A)	(B)	(C)	(D)	(E)
censure	cents	sense	sensor	censor

The repeated breaches of protocol led the chair of the meeting to propose a formal vote of ▬▬▬ on Michael, to bring him to his senses.

This is the end of the training session.
Read the explanations at the back. In the box below, note any words you came across that were unfamiliar, together with a meaning or an example of usage. Practice using these words with adults.

Word	A short sentence *you* have created, using the word

Training Session 20

Matching Words

Identify which word is MOST SIMILAR in meaning to the word on the left. Each question has only one best answer. For each question shade your one chosen answer.

		A	B	C	D	E
1	**prophesy**	ejection	omen	soothsaying	predict	extrapolation
2	**potent**	container	warning	strong	necessary	sign
3	**conspire**	sweat	overwhelm	exaggerate	plot	pyramid
4	**abundance**	profusion	resilience	bakery	disappearance	cavort
5	**ample**	loudness	double	test	plentiful	supply
6	**portion**	a lot	analogy	allot	antonym	origin
7	**obscure**	heal	inspect	recover	rectangular	uncertain

Opposite Words

Identify which word is MOST OPPOSITE in meaning to the word on the left. Each question has only one best answer. For each question shade your one chosen answer.

		A	B	C	D	E
8	**ephemeral**	profound	eternal	trivial	microscopic	individual
9	**credence**	stillness	logic	sleepiness	innocence	disbelief

Words That Do Not Match

Identify which of the 5 options A-E matches LEAST WELL in meaning to the word on the left. There is only one best answer. Shade your one chosen answer.

		A	B	C	D	E
10	**ingenuous**	innocent	inventive	childlike	unguarded	trusting
11	**scrutinise**	investigate	examine	study	incorporate	assess

Odd One Out

Each group has four words which can have similar meanings, and one word which is different. Find the odd one out. Shade your one chosen answer.

	A	B	C	D	E
12	lofty	tall	high	elevated	aloof
13	liking	affinity	learning	sympathy	leaning

Go to the next page 

14

(A)	(B)	(C)	(D)	(E)
villain	accuracy	swindler	cheat	rogue

15

(A)	(B)	(C)	(D)	(E)
thimble	brisk	alert	swift	nimble

16

(A)	(B)	(C)	(D)	(E)
rule	domination	control	authority	demand

17

(A)	(B)	(C)	(D)	(E)
continue	perpetuate	maintain	sustain	indefinite

Find The Missing Letters

Complete the sentence by identifying the missing letters. Write one letter into each of the large boxes below. After writing each letter, shade its corresponding element in the A-Z block beside it.

18 Noise from the late night party next door should have been annoying but, try as he might, Tim could not help his foot beginning to tap to the catchy r☐☐☐☐m of the drum beat.

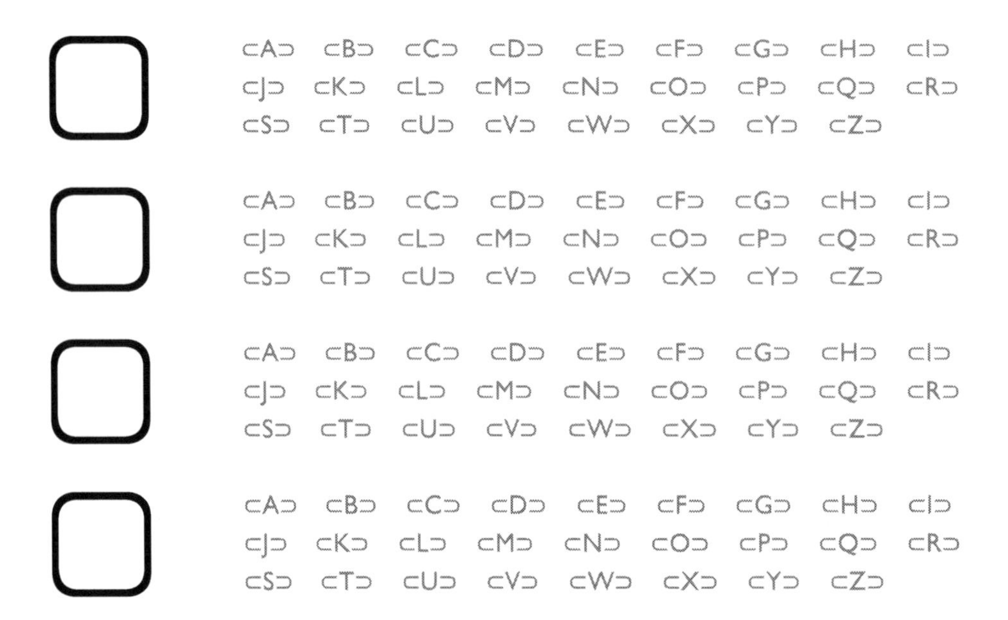

Similar relationships

Each sentence below states that one relationship is similar to another relationship. Choose the word, from options A to E, that completes the sentence best.

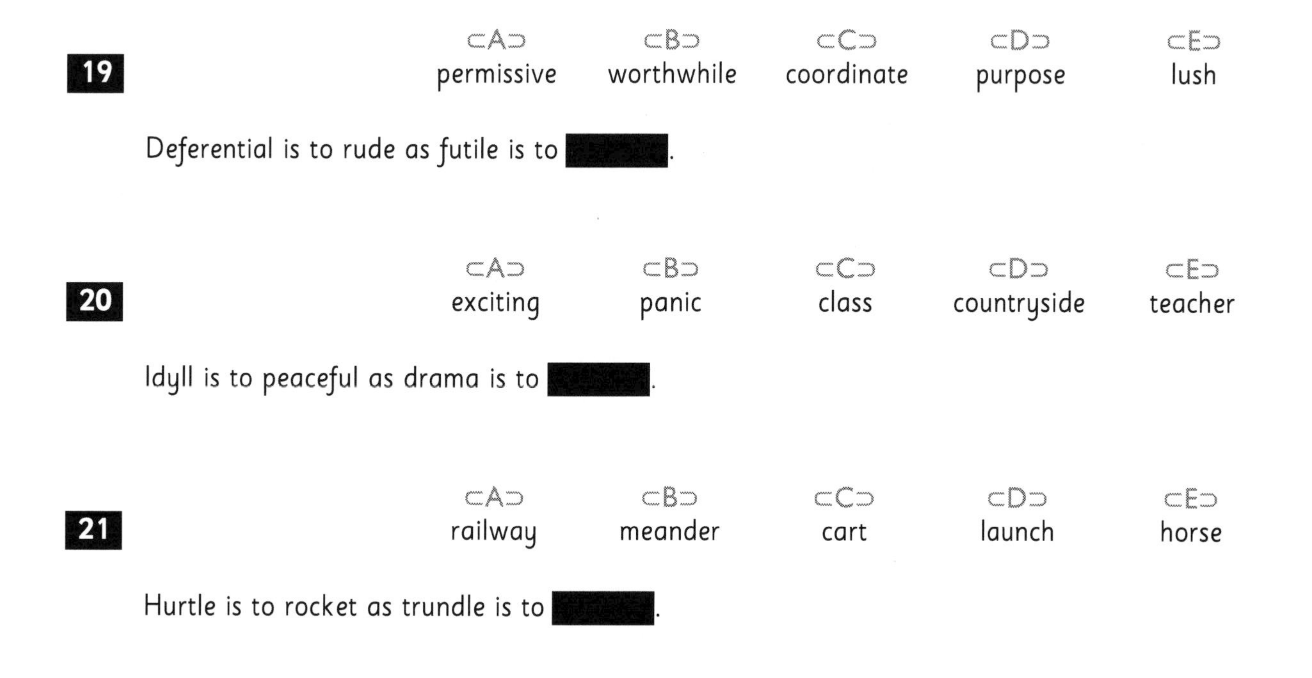

19

A	B	C	D	E
permissive	worthwhile	coordinate	purpose	lush

Deferential is to rude as futile is to ______.

20

A	B	C	D	E
exciting	panic	class	countryside	teacher

Idyll is to peaceful as drama is to ______.

21

A	B	C	D	E
railway	meander	cart	launch	horse

Hurtle is to rocket as trundle is to ______.

Find The Missing Word

In each of the following pieces of text, one word is missing.
Complete it by choosing the one option A to E which fits best.

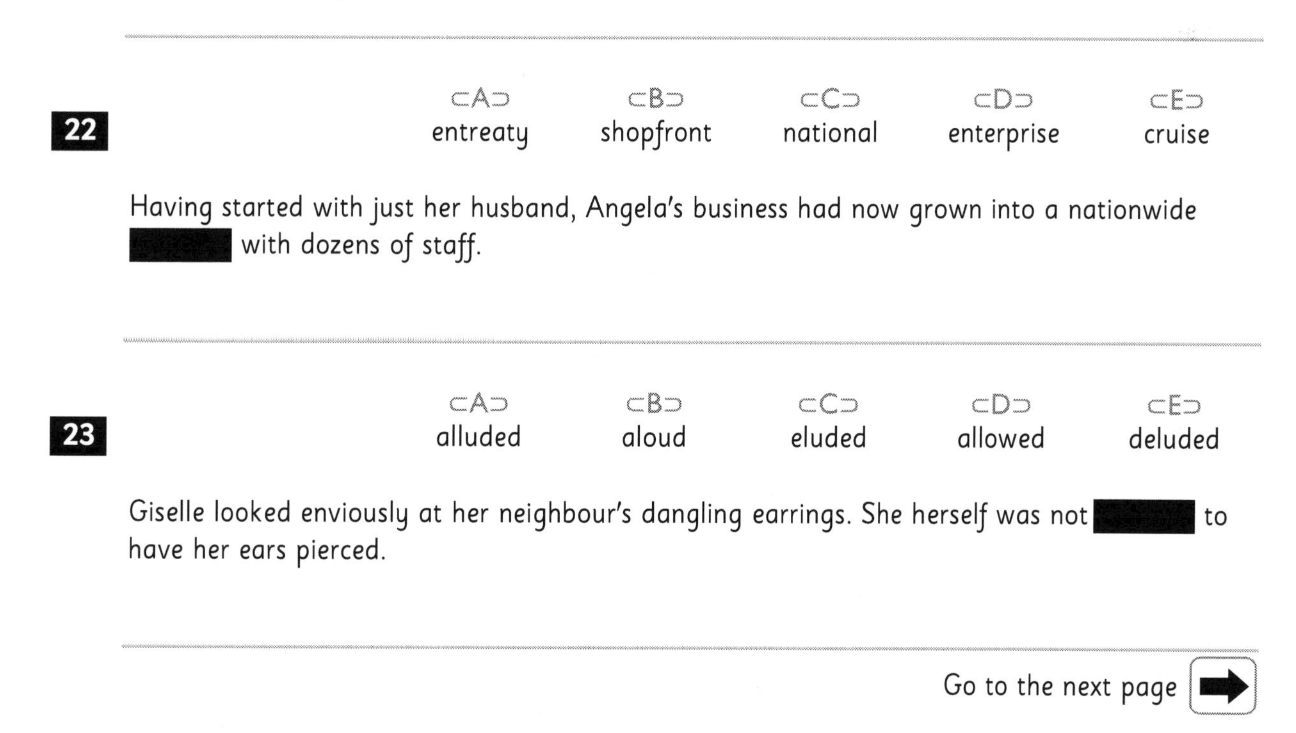

22

A	B	C	D	E
entreaty	shopfront	national	enterprise	cruise

Having started with just her husband, Angela's business had now grown into a nationwide ______ with dozens of staff.

23

A	B	C	D	E
alluded	aloud	eluded	allowed	deluded

Giselle looked enviously at her neighbour's dangling earrings. She herself was not ______ to have her ears pierced.

Go to the next page

24

⊂A⊃	⊂B⊃	⊂C⊃	⊂D⊃	⊂E⊃
mistaken	endure	replace	procrastinate	curtail

I am sorry to _____ your rejoicing at the team's success, but it is now past midnight and the neighbours will surely complain if it carries on.

25

⊂A⊃	⊂B⊃	⊂C⊃	⊂D⊃	⊂E⊃
fruit	bosom	blossom	summer	bliss

The tree survived the winter and we were relieved in spring to see it come into healthy _____.

26

⊂A⊃	⊂B⊃	⊂C⊃	⊂D⊃	⊂E⊃
acronym	synonym	synagogue	antonym	eponym

Victoria Falls gained its _____ when Scottish explorer David Livingstone saw it in 1855 in the reign of Queen Victoria. This name is now more famous than the name used by the local inhabitants of the time, Mosi-oa-Tunya.

27

⊂A⊃	⊂B⊃	⊂C⊃	⊂D⊃	⊂E⊃
convention	clamour	corral	cushion	accusation

If we took the "MyPhone 10" off the market just because a few batteries have unfortunately exploded, there would be a terrible _____ from fans who would be deprived of the enjoyment of these world-class devices.

28

⊂A⊃	⊂B⊃	⊂C⊃	⊂D⊃	⊂E⊃
womans	women	woman's	women's	womens

Sadly, the three _____ stylish dinner at the Paramount hotel was disrupted by an untimely power cut, plunging them into darkness.

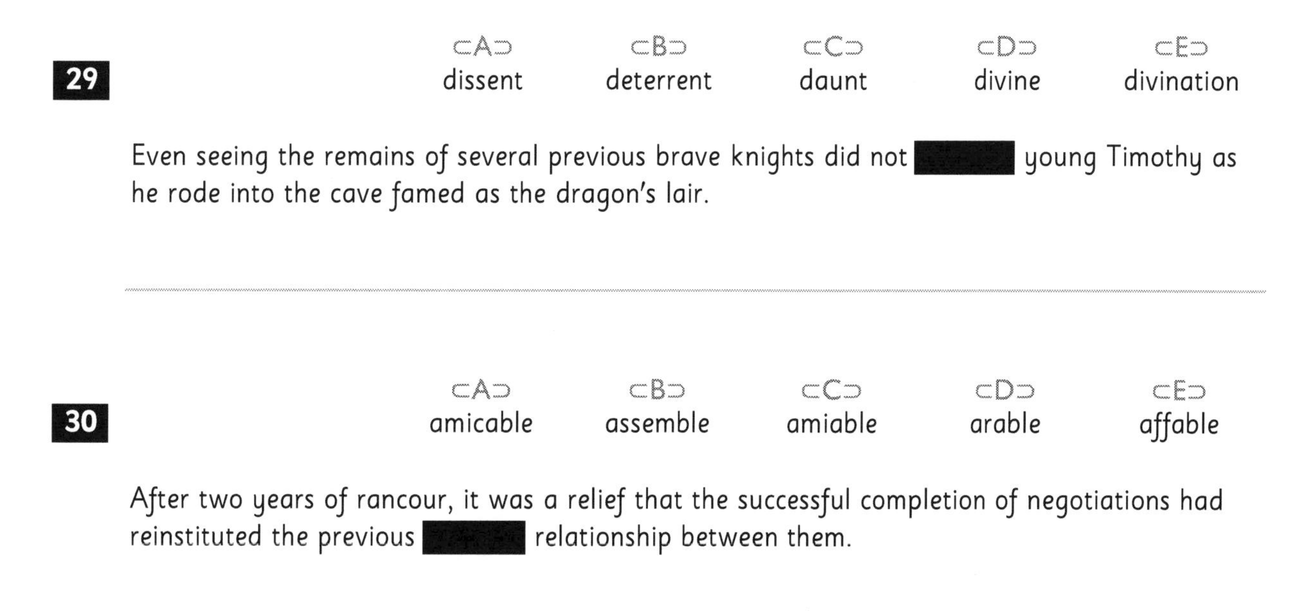

29

A	B	C	D	E
dissent	deterrent	daunt	divine	divination

Even seeing the remains of several previous brave knights did not ______ young Timothy as he rode into the cave famed as the dragon's lair.

30

A	B	C	D	E
amicable	assemble	amiable	arable	affable

After two years of rancour, it was a relief that the successful completion of negotiations had reinstituted the previous ______ relationship between them.

This is the end of the training session.

Read the explanations at the back. In the box below, note any words you came across that were unfamiliar, together with a meaning or an example of usage. Practice using these words with adults.

Word	A short sentence *you* have created, using the word

Training Session 21

Matching Words

Identify which word is MOST SIMILAR in meaning to the word on the left. Each question has only one best answer. For each question shade your one chosen answer.

		A	B	C	D	E
1	**temperate**	ferocious	overheated	momentary	restrained	corrupt
2	**judicious**	luscious	definitive	hostile	discerning	laughable
3	**pathetic**	minuscule	harmless	exaggerated	pitiful	notorious
4	**inhabit**	repeat	occupy	standardise	delay	automatic
5	**temporary**	passing	heater	hasten	coolness	speed
6	**withhold**	retain	sustain	constrict	grip	depress
7	**pensive**	payment	contemplative	delighted	accessible	outdated

Opposite Words

Identify which word is MOST OPPOSITE in meaning to the word on the left. Each question has only one best answer. For each question shade your one chosen answer.

		A	B	C	D	E
8	**enigmatic**	easy	uniform	theatrical	impractical	dramatic
9	**expedite**	retard	convert	ascend	commend	damage

Words That Do Not Match

Identify which of the 5 options A-E matches LEAST WELL in meaning to the word on the left. There is only one best answer. Shade your one chosen answer.

		A	B	C	D	E
10	**refuse**	decline	agree	garbage	rebuff	waste
11	**umpire**	referee	cross	adjudicator	judge	supervise

Odd One Out

Each group has four words which can have similar meanings, and one word which is different. Find the odd one out. Shade your one chosen answer.

	A	B	C	D	E
12	insolvent	inactive	indolent	lazy	idle
13	survive	outlive	persist	abdicate	continue

Go to the next page 

14

(A)	(B)	(C)	(D)	(E)
suppose	guess	conjecture	suspect	prisoner

15

(A)	(B)	(C)	(D)	(E)
sour	sulky	morose	moose	surly

16

(A)	(B)	(C)	(D)	(E)
satisfactorily	sufficiently	capability	competently	adequately

17

(A)	(B)	(C)	(D)	(E)
unpretentious	meek	minimalist	humble	polite

Find The Missing Letters

Complete the sentence by identifying the missing letters. Write one letter into each of the large boxes below. After writing each letter, shade its corresponding element in the A-Z block beside it.

18 As they emerged into the moonlight, the e□□□e silence became progressively more unsettling with every step.

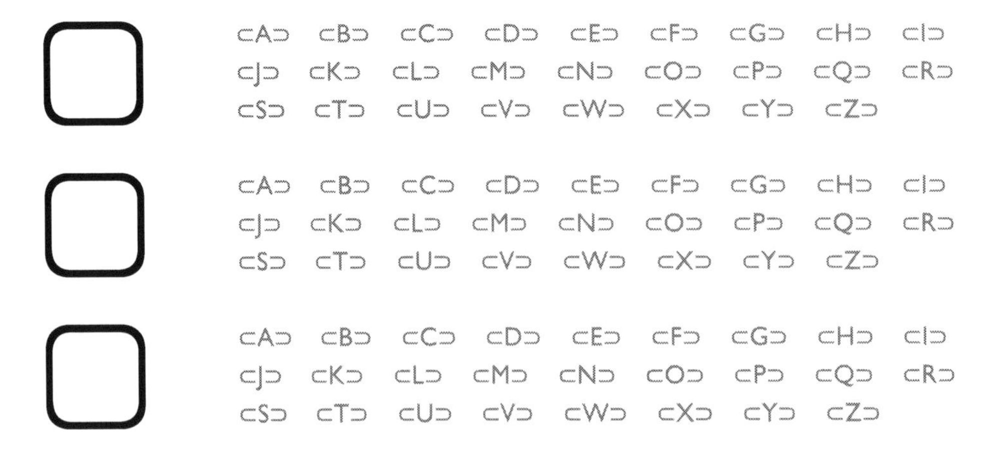

Similar relationships

Each sentence below states that one relationship is similar to another relationship. Choose the word, *from* options A to E, that completes the sentence best.

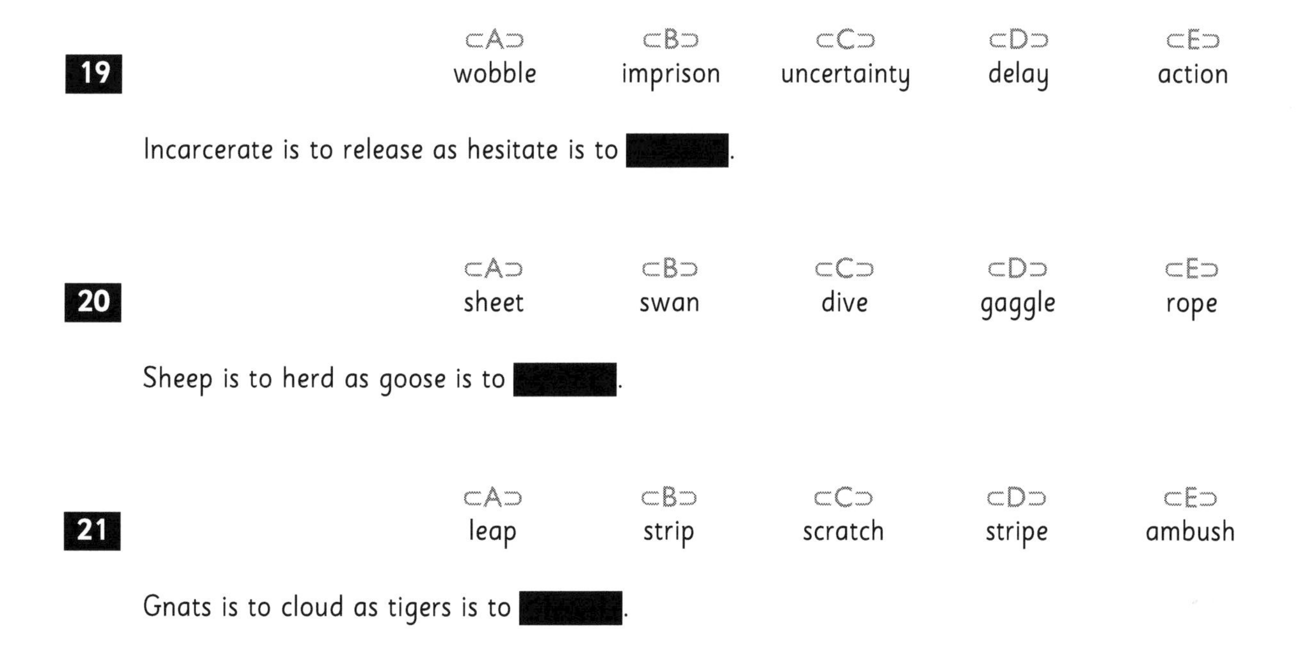

19

A	B	C	D	E
wobble	imprison	uncertainty	delay	action

Incarcerate is to release as hesitate is to ____.

20

A	B	C	D	E
sheet	swan	dive	gaggle	rope

Sheep is to herd as goose is to ____.

21

A	B	C	D	E
leap	strip	scratch	stripe	ambush

Gnats is to cloud as tigers is to ____.

Find The Missing Word

In each of the following pieces of text, one word is missing.
Complete it by choosing the one option A to E which fits best.

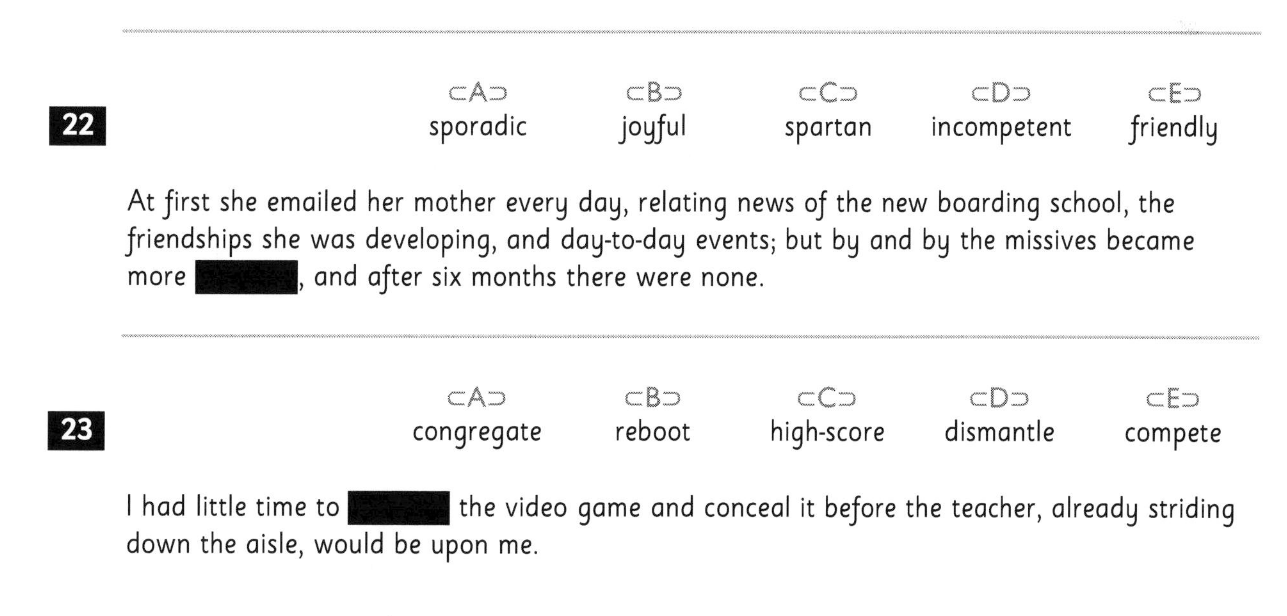

22

A	B	C	D	E
sporadic	joyful	spartan	incompetent	friendly

At first she emailed her mother every day, relating news of the new boarding school, the friendships she was developing, and day-to-day events; but by and by the missives became more ____, and after six months there were none.

23

A	B	C	D	E
congregate	reboot	high-score	dismantle	compete

I had little time to ____ the video game and conceal it before the teacher, already striding down the aisle, would be upon me.

Go to the next page

24

A	B	C	D	E
column	staircase	story	elevator	storey

An unusual feature of this building was that each ______ had its own unique colour scheme, meaning that occupants could easily identify their level within it without looking at signage.

25

A	B	C	D	E
capitol	panicked	scrutinised	capital	collapse

Security guards raced around the ______ but the president could not be found anywhere in the building.

26

A	B	C	D	E
themed	double-dealing	stoical	bittersweet	temperamental

Including a dramatic breakup of the leading couple and their later emotional reconciliation, this film was a masterpiece of ______ romance.

27

A	B	C	D	E
polarised	grizzly	polish	grisly	pole

We were astonished to be disturbed by a huge ______ bear making its way slowly through our camp.

28

A	B	C	D	E
epilogue	estimate	epidemic	epilepsy	epiphany

Month after month the team toiled in vain to build the perfect semiconductor, until one engineer, having worked two days and nights without sleep, had an ______.

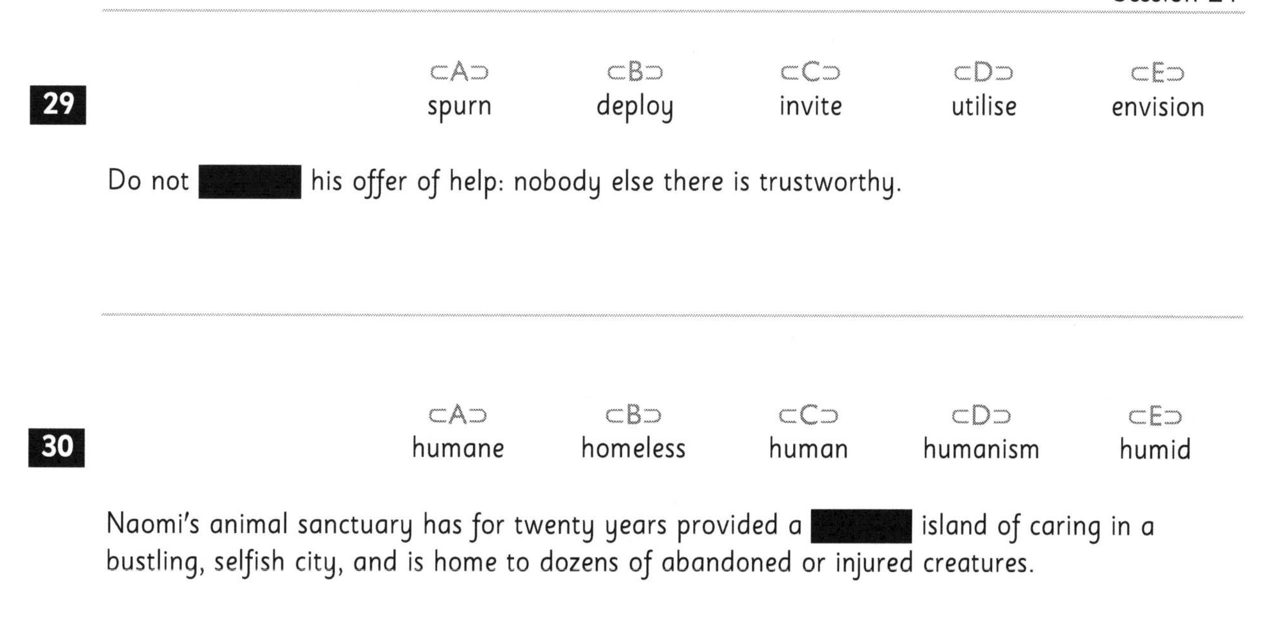

29

A	B	C	D	E
spurn	deploy	invite	utilise	envision

Do not ______ his offer of help: nobody else there is trustworthy.

30

A	B	C	D	E
humane	homeless	human	humanism	humid

Naomi's animal sanctuary has for twenty years provided a ______ island of caring in a bustling, selfish city, and is home to dozens of abandoned or injured creatures.

This is the end of the training session.
Read the explanations at the back. In the box below, note any words you came across that were unfamiliar, together with a meaning or an example of usage. Practice using these words with adults.

Word	A short sentence *you* have created, using the word

Training Session 22

Matching Words

Identify which word is MOST SIMILAR in meaning to the word on the left. Each question has only one best answer. For each question shade your one chosen answer.

		A	B	C	D	E
1	**suspend**	spring	dangle	flicker	reinstate	discipline
2	**sluggish**	tasteless	bulbous	slimy	lethargic	baggage
3	**significance**	selection	weight	originality	digit	form
4	**insolent**	stocking	island	impertinent	bankrupt	prevent
5	**illicit**	forbidden	saliva	cause	budget	obtain
6	**indulge**	swelling	nappy	encourage	boathouse	pamper
7	**sacred**	marked	sweetened	divine	violet	terrified

Opposite Words

Identify which word is MOST OPPOSITE in meaning to the word on the left. Each question has only one best answer. For each question shade your one chosen answer.

		A	B	C	D	E
8	**discerning**	off-centre	appearing	fair-minded	unselective	stationary
9	**gung-ho**	hesitant	disappeared	enthusiastic	vicious	uninitiated

Words That Do Not Match

Identify which of the 5 options A-E matches LEAST WELL in meaning to the word on the left. There is only one best answer. Shade your one chosen answer.

		A	B	C	D	E
10	**approve**	esteem	praise	register	appreciate	commend
11	**anxious**	concerned	nervous	envious	disturbed	apprehensive

Odd One Out

Each group has four words which can have similar meanings, and one word which is different. Find the odd one out. Shade your one chosen answer.

	A	B	C	D	E
12	submissive	subtracting	unassuming	self-effacing	unassertive
13	unkempt	incompetent	inept	bungling	inane

Go to the next page 

14 (A) swagger (B) parade (C) ceremony (D) strut (E) flourish

15 (A) plan (B) policy (C) substance (D) strategy (E) scheme

16 (A) morale (B) honest (C) good (D) ethical (E) virtuous

17 (A) store (B) hold (C) reserve (D) retain (E) exploit

Find The Missing Letters

Complete the sentence by identifying the missing letters. Write one letter into each of the large boxes below. After writing each letter, shade its corresponding element in the A-Z block beside it.

18 It is no good reassuring me that the dog has never harmed anyone. It has f□□□□e eyes and ferocious teeth, and it is already posturing as if to attack.

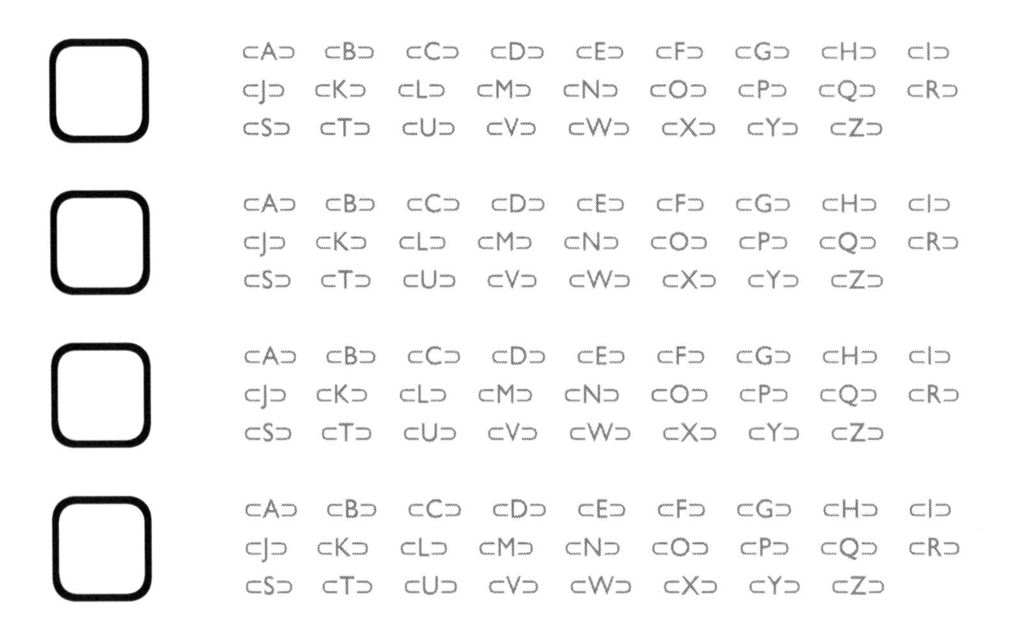

Similar relationships

Each sentence below states that one relationship is similar to another relationship. Choose the word, from options A to E, that completes the sentence best.

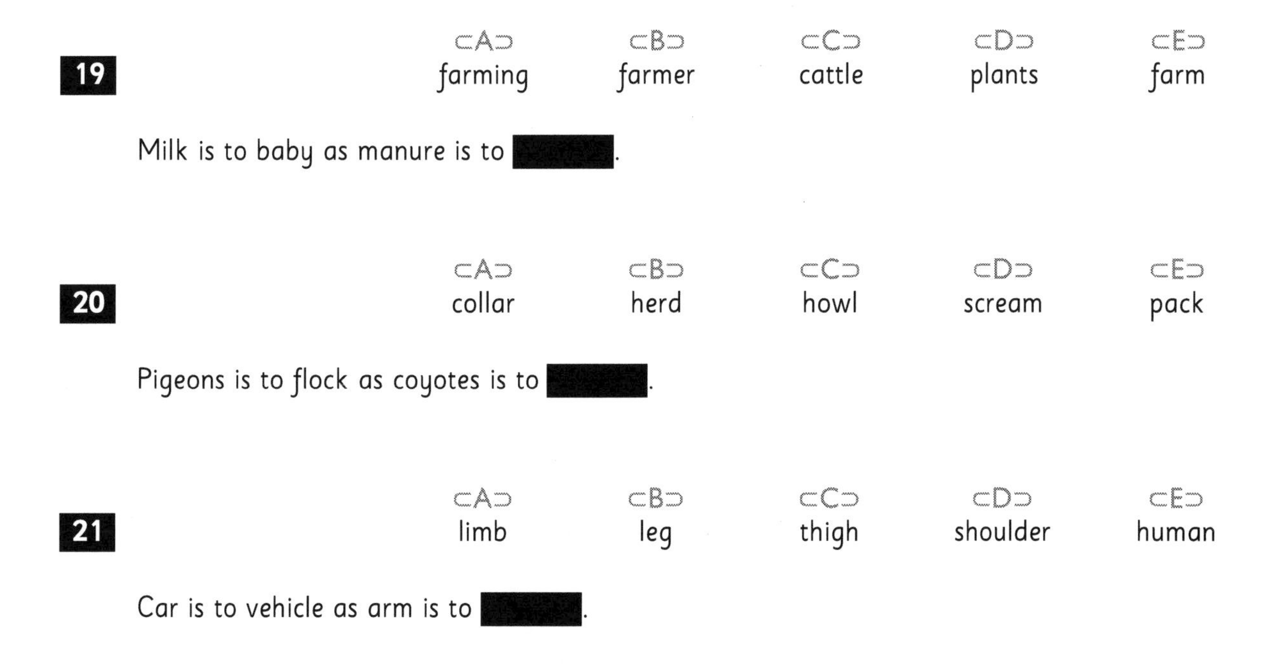

19

A	B	C	D	E
farming	farmer	cattle	plants	farm

Milk is to baby as manure is to _____.

20

A	B	C	D	E
collar	herd	howl	scream	pack

Pigeons is to flock as coyotes is to _____.

21

A	B	C	D	E
limb	leg	thigh	shoulder	human

Car is to vehicle as arm is to _____.

Find The Missing Word

In each of the following pieces of text, one word is missing.
Complete it by choosing the one option A to E which fits best.

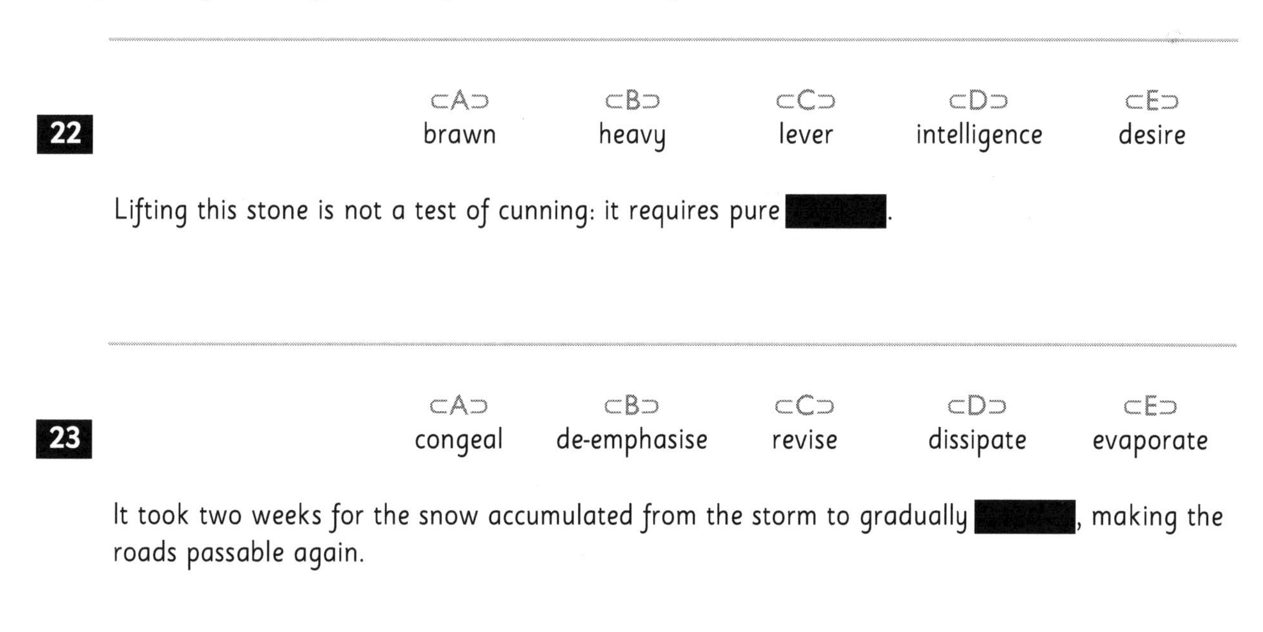

22

A	B	C	D	E
brawn	heavy	lever	intelligence	desire

Lifting this stone is not a test of cunning: it requires pure _____.

23

A	B	C	D	E
congeal	de-emphasise	revise	dissipate	evaporate

It took two weeks for the snow accumulated from the storm to gradually _____, making the roads passable again.

Go to the next page

24

A	B	C	D	E
inhibition	exhibition	dramatization	devastation	discontent

Even half an hour into the play, there were already signs of ▇▇▇ amongst the audience: heads were bobbing and feet were shuffling.

25

A	B	C	D	E
insignificant	differential	delinquent	effervescence	insouciance

I agree that Gavin deserves a higher salary for doing a much more complicated job, but this degree of pay ▇▇▇ is just ridiculous.

26

A	B	C	D	E
sent	cent	censure	censor	sensor

I never intended to ▇▇▇ the student magazine, but it is simply not acceptable to use it to lampoon a teacher in this way.

27

A	B	C	D	E
mollify	degrade	improve	bicycle	mark

Year after year of sugary drinks and frequent omission of tooth brushing has inevitably caused your tooth enamel to ▇▇▇ substantially.

28

A	B	C	D	E
cancel	shattered	council	desperate	counsel

At a terrible time like this, as you know, I would always come to you for ▇▇▇. This has always been helpful in the past and I hope it will be so again now.

29

A	B	C	D	E
hot	handsome	delicious	bland	gruesome

I was looking forward to us having something spicy at the curry house. I had no idea it would be so disappointingly ______. It later emerged that my sister, who dislikes spices, had telephoned ahead to arrange this as a special request.

30

A	B	C	D	E
customer	virtual	awful	patronising	fishing

When I asked a simple question, I was disappointed to be greeted with a ______ response, a far poorer level of service than I expected.

This is the end of the training session.

Read the explanations at the back. In the box below, note any words you came across that were unfamiliar, together with a meaning or an example of usage. Practice using these words with adults.

Word	A short sentence *you* have created, using the word

Training Session 23

Matching Words

Identify which word is MOST SIMILAR in meaning to the word on the left. Each question has only one best answer. For each question shade your one chosen answer.

		A	B	C	D	E
1	**altitude**	elevation	distance	rudeness	angle	approach
2	**assemble**	congregate	realise	attach	imagine	liken
3	**surpass**	astonish	outdo	document	motorway	bridge
4	**prophecy**	instinct	prediction	futuristic	foretell	expect
5	**testimony**	conversation	possession	statement	unwieldy	examination
6	**propriety**	possession	ownership	curiosity	decency	building
7	**rudimentary**	insolent	molested	irritating	report	basic

Opposite Words

Identify which word is MOST OPPOSITE in meaning to the word on the left. Each question has only one best answer. For each question shade your one chosen answer.

		A	B	C	D	E
8	**praise**	ignominy	ugly	defame	hatred	shambolic
9	**impress**	reschedule	dismiss	relocate	underwhelm	redesign

Words That Do Not Match

Identify which of the 5 options A-E matches LEAST WELL in meaning to the word on the left. There is only one best answer. Shade your one chosen answer.

		A	B	C	D	E
10	**distribute**	arrange	apportion	dispense	mete	apprehensive
11	**appease**	calm	serve	reward	placate	fill

Odd One Out

Each group has four words which can have similar meanings, and one word which is different. Find the odd one out. Shade your one chosen answer.

	A	B	C	D	E
12	emotionless	irascible	tranquil	unruffled	composed
13	desire	stimulus	insistence	motive	spur

Go to the next page 

14

(A)	(B)	(C)	(D)	(E)
stark	plain	barren	empty	bear

15

(A)	(B)	(C)	(D)	(E)
reticent	inhibited	restrained	reluctant	withdrawn

16

(A)	(B)	(C)	(D)	(E)
cheap	stable	fixed	safe	solid

17

(A)	(B)	(C)	(D)	(E)
exhaust	conserve	consume	deplete	squander

Find The Missing Letters

Complete the sentence by identifying the missing letters. Write one letter into each of the large boxes below. After writing each letter, shade its corresponding element in the A-Z block beside it.

18 This is the slowest rest□□□□nt I have ever had the displeasure to dine in. Some people's meals have gone cold while they waited politely for the meals of others to arrive. The only thing that was quick to arrive was the bill.

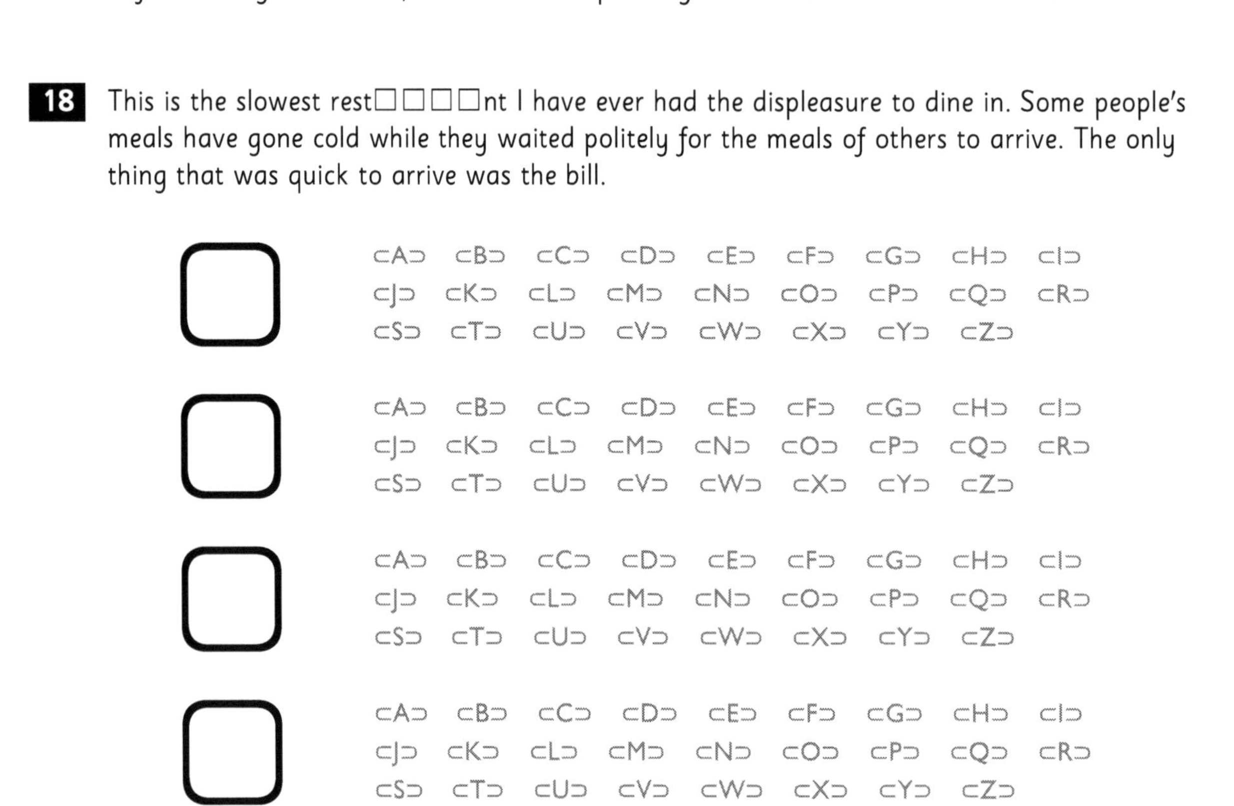

Similar relationships

Each sentence below states that one relationship is similar to another relationship. Choose the word, from options A to E, that completes the sentence best.

19

A	B	C	D	E
fill	mine	yours	rotate	spade

Attack is to retreat as dig is to ______.

20

A	B	C	D	E
herd	spray	leap	pod	rejuvenation

Frogs is to army as dolphins is to ______.

21

A	B	C	D	E
nose	mouth	eye	smile	ear

Nail is to finger as lobe is to ______.

Find The Missing Word

In each of the following pieces of text, one word is missing.
Complete it by choosing the one option A to E which fits best.

22

A	B	C	D	E
foreign	course	furry	frowny	coarse

In front of these very young children, I will thank you to avoid using any such ______ language.

23

A	B	C	D	E
child	child's	children	childrens	children's

Extreme heat this year was a great impediment to the ______ concentration during their exams.

Go to the next page

24

⊂A⊃	⊂B⊃	⊂C⊃	⊂D⊃	⊂E⊃
both	birth	berth	breath	broth

After waving goodbye to their grandchildren who had come to the port to see them off on their cruise, Glenda and Daniel made their way up to their ______ on the upper deck of the liner.

25

⊂A⊃	⊂B⊃	⊂C⊃	⊂D⊃	⊂E⊃
conceal	disseminate	instigate	repeal	deviate

We should ______ the good news as widely as possible, and be careful to ensure that the credit for our achievement comes to us and not just our parents.

26

⊂A⊃	⊂B⊃	⊂C⊃	⊂D⊃	⊂E⊃
extended	emergency	splendid	amateurish	longer

A short visit does not do justice to the majesty of Bali's wilderness. It is necessary to take an ______ vacation to really grasp its splendour.

27

⊂A⊃	⊂B⊃	⊂C⊃	⊂D⊃	⊂E⊃
recognised	unconscious	frequent	intentional	international

As she walked past the ice cream parlour, she experienced - or so she later said - an ______ drift in her footsteps that led her, seemingly accidentally, inside the building and then onward to the milkshake machine.

28

⊂A⊃	⊂B⊃	⊂C⊃	⊂D⊃	⊂E⊃
cored	chore	chord	core	cord

After the devastating collision, the doctors were very concerned that there had been injury to his spinal ______.

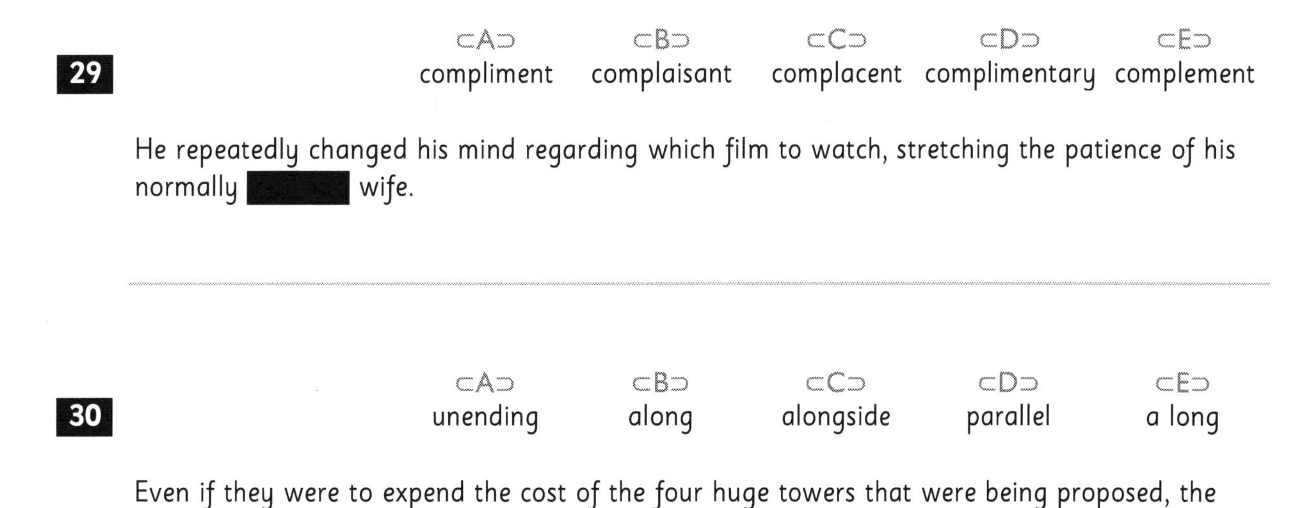

29

A	B	C	D	E
compliment	complaisant	complacent	complimentary	complement

He repeatedly changed his mind regarding which film to watch, stretching the patience of his normally ▆▆▆▆ wife.

30

A	B	C	D	E
unending	along	alongside	parallel	a long

Even if they were to expend the cost of the four huge towers that were being proposed, the distance from each tower to the next would still need to be spanned by ▆▆▆▆ causeway.

This is the end of the training session.
Read the explanations at the back. In the box below, note any words you came across that were unfamiliar, together with a meaning or an example of usage. Practice using these words with adults.

Word	A short sentence *you* have created, using the word

Training Session 24

Matching Words

Identify which word is MOST SIMILAR in meaning to the word on the left. Each question has only one best answer. For each question shade your one chosen answer.

		A	B	C	D	E
1	**idiosyncrasy**	foolishness	simultaneity	peculiarity	regularity	equivalence
2	**exult**	worship	depart	impress	rejoice	revere
3	**mundane**	annual	daily	heavenly	weekly	dull
4	**subdued**	deducted	inverted	sombre	industrious	laughable
5	**determine**	underground	terminate	restart	branch	ascertain
6	**prevalent**	neighbourly	refuse	classy	blushing	common
7	**valiant**	expensive	shining	efficient	brave	dependent

Opposite Words

Identify which word is MOST OPPOSITE in meaning to the word on the left. Each question has only one best answer. For each question shade your one chosen answer.

		A	B	C	D	E
8	**exonerate**	convict	depress	remove	involve	stagnate
9	**exacerbate**	miniaturise	congregate	ingratiate	alleviate	subtract

Words That Do Not Match

Identify which of the 5 options A-E matches LEAST WELL in meaning to the word on the left. There is only one best answer. Shade your one chosen answer.

		A	B	C	D	E
10	**overt**	public	outward	terminate	plain	manifest
11	**parable**	similar	story	allegory	lesson	fable

Odd One Out

Each group has four words which can have similar meanings, and one word which is different. Find the odd one out. Shade your one chosen answer.

	A	B	C	D	E
12	imperfect	defective	blemished	operative	flawed
13	malice	animosity	charm	hatred	enmity

Go to the next page 

	A	B	C	D	E
14	hypothetical	supposed	diagonal	theoretical	speculative
15	distinct	pacific	discrete	particular	specific
16	stark	bleak	austere	spartan	aggressive
17	minimal	scarce	meagre	skimpy	transparent

Find The Missing Letters

Complete the sentence by identifying the missing letters. Write one letter into each of the large boxes below. After writing each letter, shade its corresponding element in the A-Z block beside it.

18 Standards of hy□□□□e in that cafe were dreadfully low, I am sorry to say. I doubted the staff could even wash their hands easily since there seemed to be no sink.

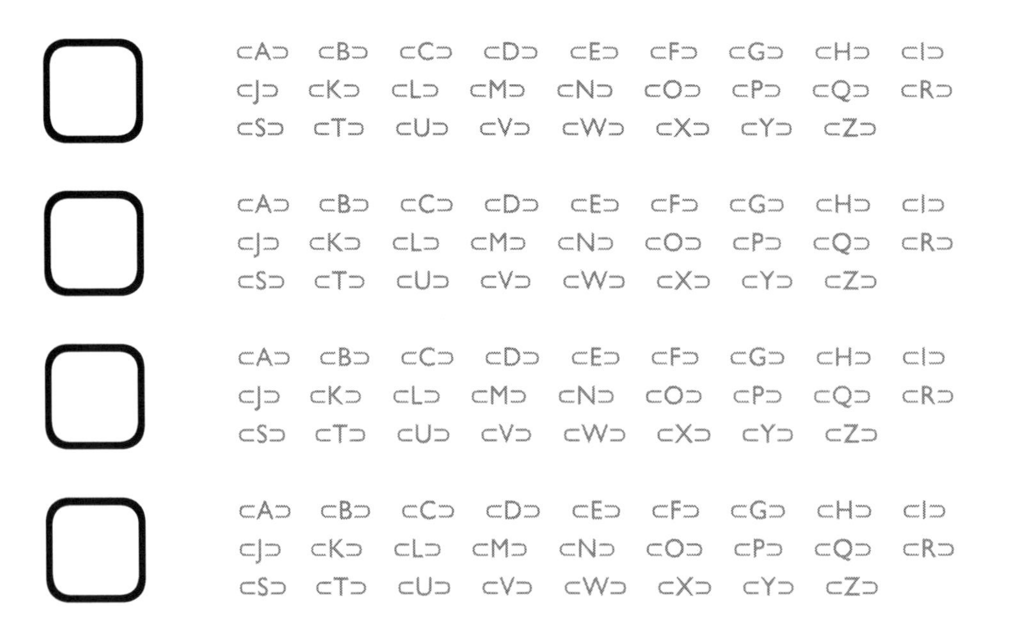

Similar relationships

Each sentence below states that one relationship is similar to another relationship. Choose the word, from options A to E, that completes the sentence best.

19

A	B	C	D	E
cascade	caravan	queue	hump	pile

People is to crowd as camel is to ______.

20

A	B	C	D	E
trousers	underpants	belt	buckle	socks

Buttons is to shirt as zip is to ______.

21

A	B	C	D	E
swarm	languor	bouquet	drift	pride

Pelicans is to pod as pheasants is to ______.

Find The Missing Word

In each of the following pieces of text, one word is missing.
Complete it by choosing the one option A to E which fits best.

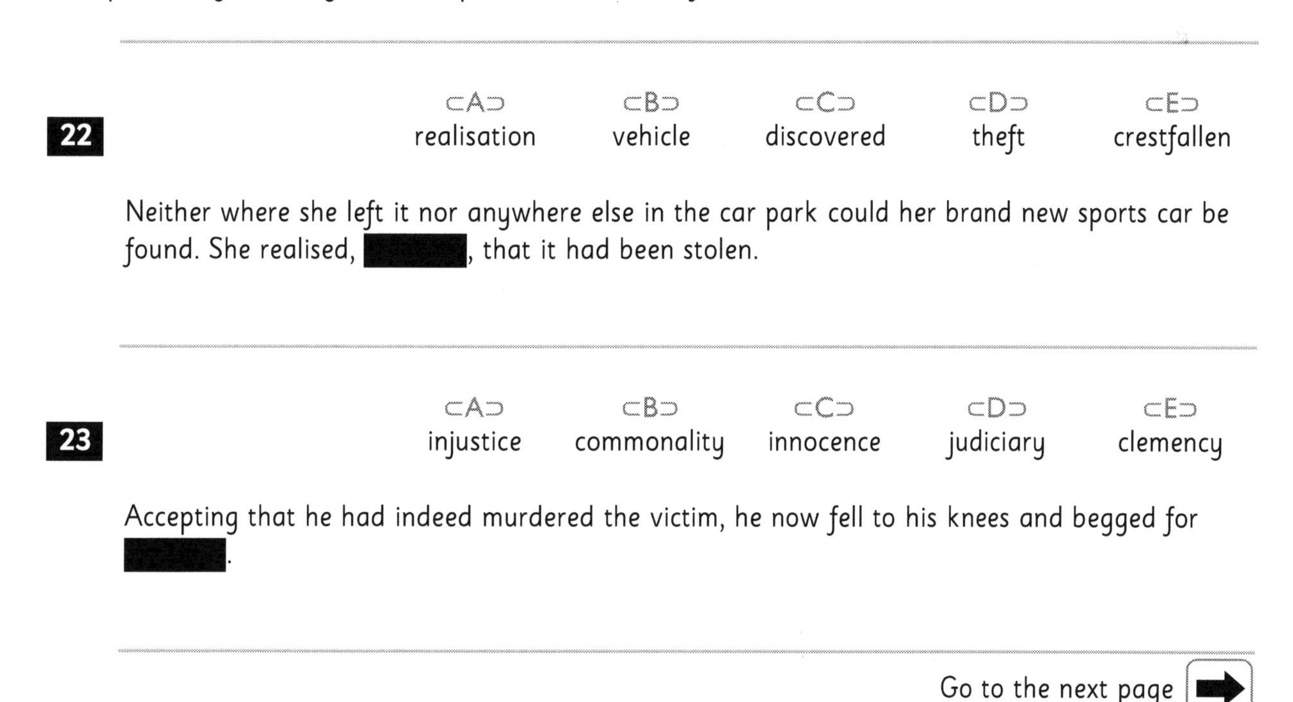

22

A	B	C	D	E
realisation	vehicle	discovered	theft	crestfallen

Neither where she left it nor anywhere else in the car park could her brand new sports car be found. She realised, ______, that it had been stolen.

23

A	B	C	D	E
injustice	commonality	innocence	judiciary	clemency

Accepting that he had indeed murdered the victim, he now fell to his knees and begged for ______.

Go to the next page

24

⊂A⊃	⊂B⊃	⊂C⊃	⊂D⊃	⊂E⊃
influential	differential	inebriated	deferential	indifferent

You were being very ______ to the examiner in the music test: are you hoping she will give you extra marks?

25

⊂A⊃	⊂B⊃	⊂C⊃	⊂D⊃	⊂E⊃
inevitable	unthinkable	rejection	warfare	acceptable

Mistreatment of prisoners, even those captured in war, is completely ______ and in any case forbidden by international law.

26

⊂A⊃	⊂B⊃	⊂C⊃	⊂D⊃	⊂E⊃
emphasis	internet	corrupt	blasphemy	temperature

In the hothouse environment of this high technology startup, any suggestion that our new website might not actually be particularly useful was treated as ______.

27

⊂A⊃	⊂B⊃	⊂C⊃	⊂D⊃	⊂E⊃
dispute	camaraderie	admonish	beautiful	enjoyment

Jointly facing the same enormous delays at the airport, the passengers on all the flights developed a gratifying sense of ______.

28

⊂A⊃	⊂B⊃	⊂C⊃	⊂D⊃	⊂E⊃
drain	levy	pay	contribute	augment

To pay for the forthcoming war, the new government decided it would ______ a new tax on car tyres, including the spare tyre.

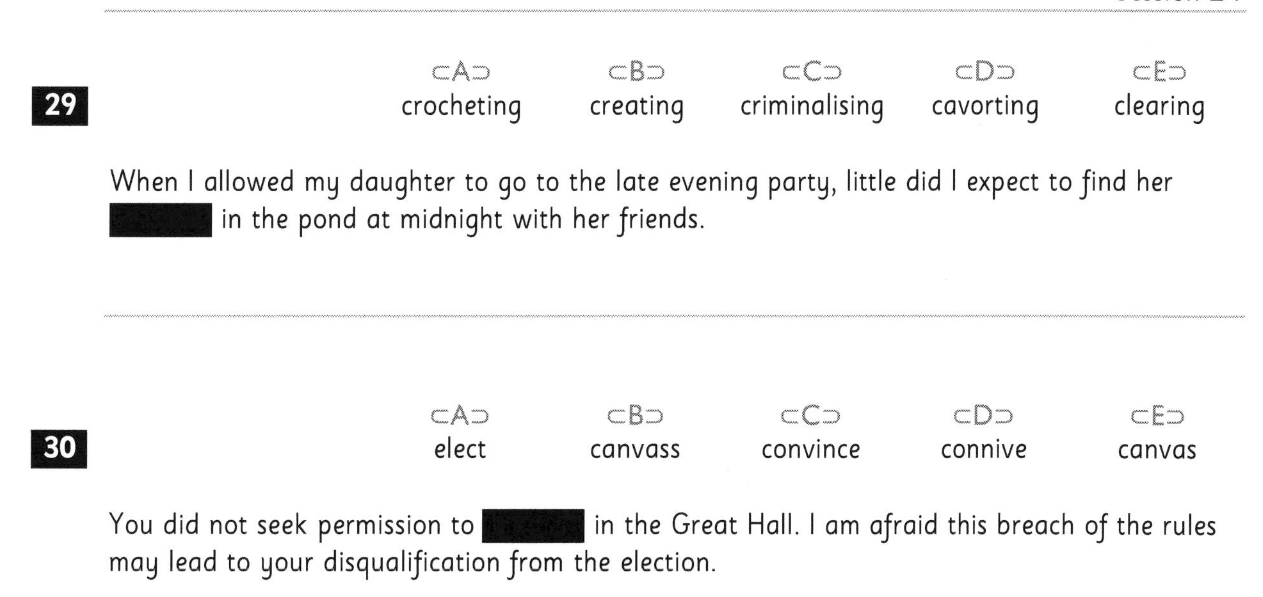

29

⊂A⊃	⊂B⊃	⊂C⊃	⊂D⊃	⊂E⊃
crocheting	creating	criminalising	cavorting	clearing

When I allowed my daughter to go to the late evening party, little did I expect to find her ______ in the pond at midnight with her friends.

30

⊂A⊃	⊂B⊃	⊂C⊃	⊂D⊃	⊂E⊃
elect	canvass	convince	connive	canvas

You did not seek permission to ______ in the Great Hall. I am afraid this breach of the rules may lead to your disqualification from the election.

This is the end of the training session.
Read the explanations at the back. In the box below, note any words you came across that were unfamiliar, together with a meaning or an example of usage. Practice using these words with adults.

Word	A short sentence *you* have created, using the word

Training Session 25

Matching Words

Identify which word is MOST SIMILAR in meaning to the word on the left. Each question has only one best answer. For each question shade your one chosen answer.

		A	B	C	D	E
1	**stoop**	mountain	bend	swerve	halt	apex
2	**influence**	affect	expand	queue	rinse	valuable
3	**conscious**	doubt	guilt	remorseful	contrite	aware
4	**benefit**	advantage	adjustment	tighten	disappoint	price
5	**associate**	party	friendliness	partner	enlighten	donkey
6	**inferior**	scary	warrior	untried	inside	lowly
7	**minor**	excavator	small	bird	ours	lamp

Opposite Words

Identify which word is MOST OPPOSITE in meaning to the word on the left. Each question has only one best answer. For each question shade your one chosen answer.

		A	B	C	D	E
8	**gregarious**	roofless	individualistic	outdoor	overcrowd	voluntary
9	**euphonious**	unlimited	rationed	modest	trumpeting	clashing

Words That Do Not Match

Identify which of the 5 options A-E matches LEAST WELL in meaning to the word on the left. There is only one best answer. Shade your one chosen answer.

		A	B	C	D	E
10	**sanguine**	buoyant	optimistic	confident	assured	panicked
11	**resolve**	decide	deduct	rectify	determination	settle

Odd One Out

Each group has four words which can have similar meanings, and one word which is different. Find the odd one out. Shade your one chosen answer.

	A	B	C	D	E
12	interval	hiatus	break	snap	space
13	territory	mountain	domain	jurisdiction	dominion

Go to the next page 

14 (A) competent (B) despicable (C) trustworthy (D) careful (E) reliable

15 (A) privacy (B) loneliness (C) solitude (D) isolation (E) solace

16 (A) relieving (B) comforting (C) consoling (D) calming (E) rejoicing

17 (A) enough (B) acceptable (C) satisfactory (D) pleasant (E) adequate

---

Find The Missing Letters

Complete the sentence by identifying the missing letters. Write one letter into each of the large boxes below. After writing each letter, shade its corresponding element in the A-Z block beside it.

18 Travel to for□□□□ countries can be complicated and expensive, but expands the mind and broadens one's horizons.

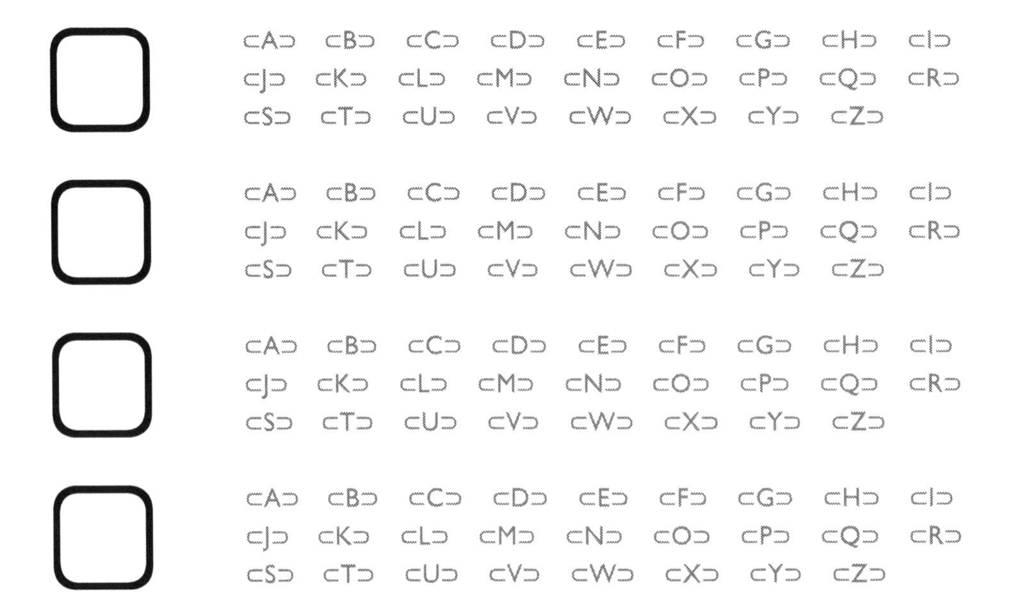

Similar relationships

Each sentence below states that one relationship is similar to another relationship. Choose the word, from options A to E, that completes the sentence best.

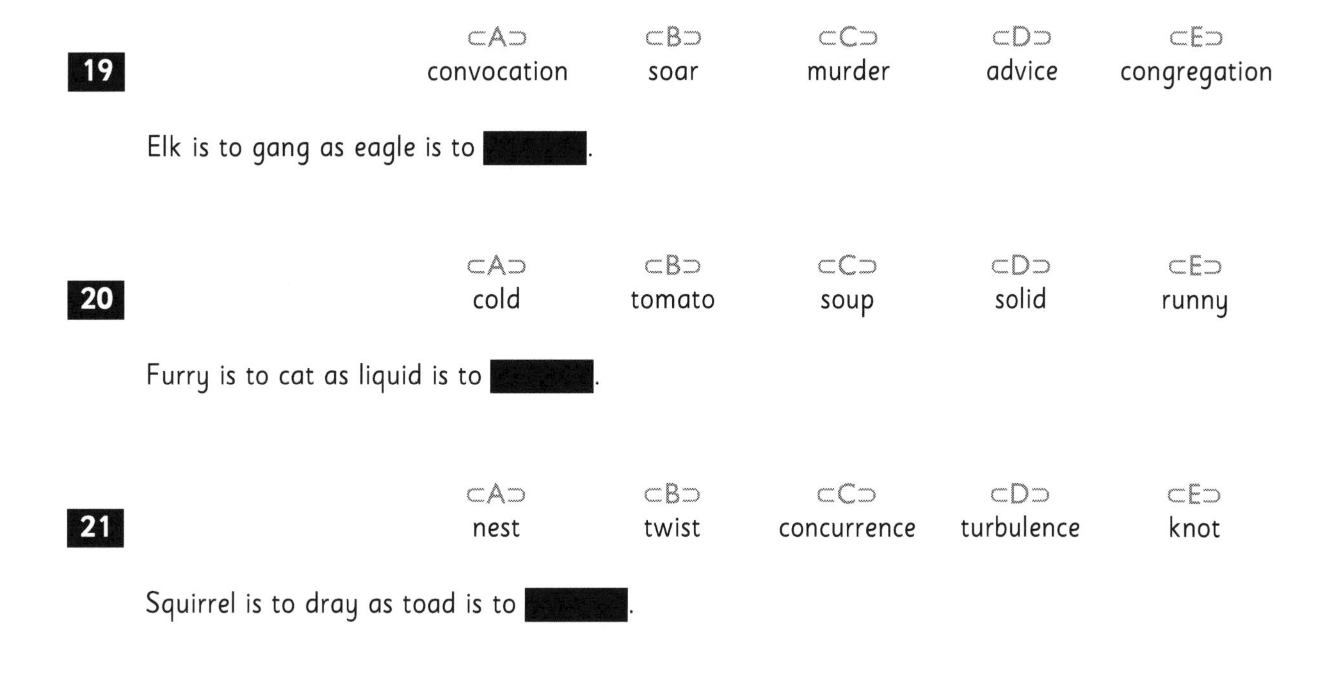

19

A	B	C	D	E
convocation	soar	murder	advice	congregation

Elk is to gang as eagle is to ______.

20

A	B	C	D	E
cold	tomato	soup	solid	runny

Furry is to cat as liquid is to ______.

21

A	B	C	D	E
nest	twist	concurrence	turbulence	knot

Squirrel is to dray as toad is to ______.

Find The Missing Word

In each of the following pieces of text, one word is missing.
Complete it by choosing the one option A to E which fits best.

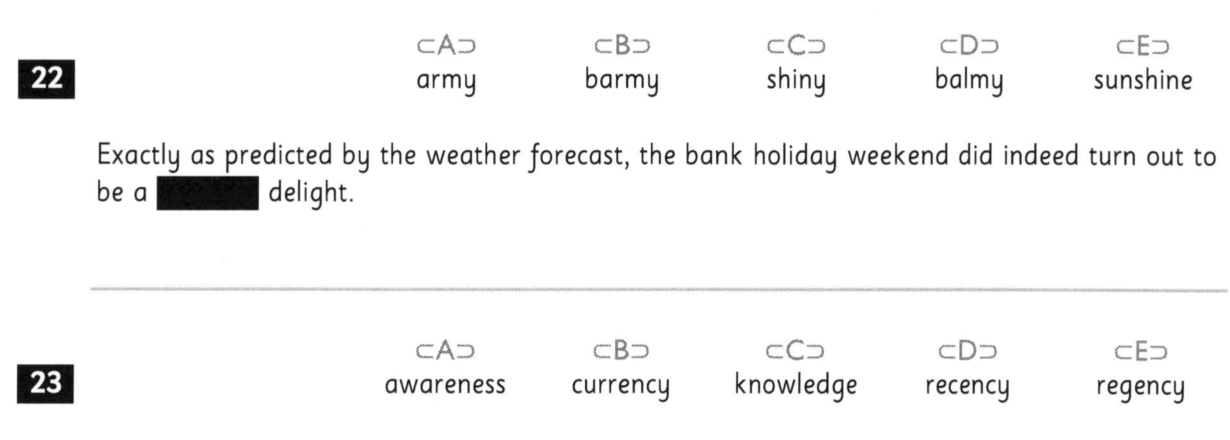

22

A	B	C	D	E
army	barmy	shiny	balmy	sunshine

Exactly as predicted by the weather forecast, the bank holiday weekend did indeed turn out to be a ______ delight.

23

A	B	C	D	E
awareness	currency	knowledge	recency	regency

It was no good having a wallet stuffed with pounds. He had no local ______ at all, and this was turning into a serious problem as he wound his sad way from one apologetic shopkeeper to the next.

Go to the next page ➡

24

⊂A⊃	⊂B⊃	⊂C⊃	⊂D⊃	⊂E⊃
calamity	fortunate	disastrous	erroneous	incompetent

Losing his mobile phone in Milan was a _____, since it contained his flight and hotel details for the remaining steps of his pan-European tour.

25

⊂A⊃	⊂B⊃	⊂C⊃	⊂D⊃	⊂E⊃
side	cite	site	sight	sighed

Your dry cleaning company has definitely damaged my clothes on several occasions in the last few months, although I cannot at this moment _____ particular examples.

26

⊂A⊃	⊂B⊃	⊂C⊃	⊂D⊃	⊂E⊃
distribute	imitate	wreath	congregate	wreathe

Don't smoke this cigar before your meeting. It will _____ you in an unpleasant odour and distract your clients.

27

⊂A⊃	⊂B⊃	⊂C⊃	⊂D⊃	⊂E⊃
two-line	rhymes	stanza	epic	tiny

Obi had spent months learning the _____ poem, and was very excited to be able to recite a fragment, in his opinion far too brief, to the class that afternoon.

28

⊂A⊃	⊂B⊃	⊂C⊃	⊂D⊃	⊂E⊃
disparity	exaggeration	disappearance	approximation	outrageous

The _____ between your estimate of the cost of this work and your actual final bill is extraordinary: it is difficult to understand how they can relate to the same work.

29

A	B	C	D	E
atheist	prayer	church	deity	triptych

The chapel was ingeniously arranged so that any worshippers could pay their respects to their chosen ████ without their gaze falling upon items, of value to other attendees, but which they might find blasphemous.

30

A	B	C	D	E
mind	paint	studio	canvass	canvas

It was only 10 days before the exhibition and all Anton had for the centrepiece was a blank ████.

This is the end of the training session.
Read the explanations at the back. In the box below, note any words you came across that were unfamiliar, together with a meaning or an example of usage. Practice using these words with adults.

Word	A short sentence *you* have created, using the word

Training Session 26

Matching Words

Identify which word is MOST SIMILAR in meaning to the word on the left. Each question has only one best answer. For each question shade your one chosen answer.

		A	B	C	D	E
1	**meticulous**	curious	convergent	ticklish	painstaking	trembling
2	**fragrant**	piece	perfumed	operative	ablaze	donated
3	**contempt**	reinitiate	association	try	tepee	scorn
4	**impudent**	weak	insulting	careless	unwise	careless
5	**incisive**	branched	toothy	overpriced	squalid	penetrating
6	**legal**	footwear	anklet	feminine	legitimate	predator
7	**ensure**	safeguard	perspire	uncertain	possible	hesitant

Opposite Words

Identify which word is MOST OPPOSITE in meaning to the word on the left. Each question has only one best answer. For each question shade your one chosen answer.

		A	B	C	D	E
8	**hackneyed**	pockmarked	refined	preplanned	original	untested
9	**public**	shameful	open	private	national	reported

Words That Do Not Match

Identify which of the 5 options A-E matches LEAST WELL in meaning to the word on the left. There is only one best answer. Shade your one chosen answer.

		A	B	C	D	E
10	**voluminous**	lengthy	copious	loose	silent	ample
11	**ramble**	waffle	thorn	hike	prattle	trek

Odd One Out

Each group has four words which can have similar meanings, and one word which is different. Find the odd one out. Shade your one chosen answer.

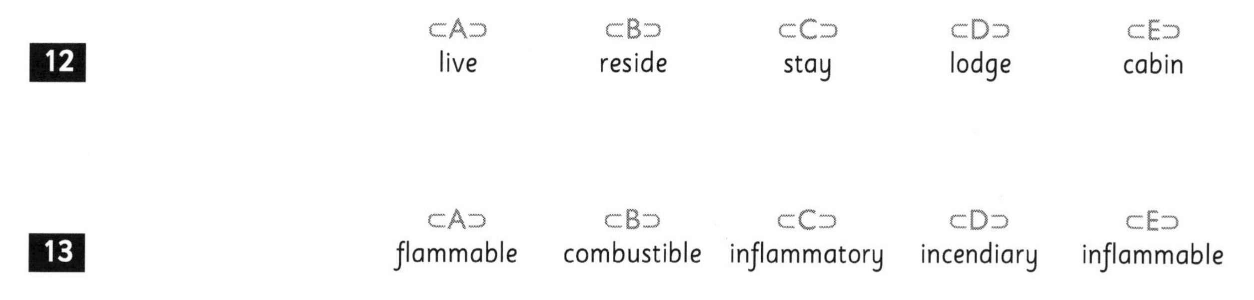

	A	B	C	D	E
12	live	reside	stay	lodge	cabin
13	flammable	combustible	inflammatory	incendiary	inflammable

Go to the next page 

14

⊂A⊃	⊂B⊃	⊂C⊃	⊂D⊃	⊂E⊃
alliance	society	union	company	business

15

⊂A⊃	⊂B⊃	⊂C⊃	⊂D⊃	⊂E⊃
subterranean	subterfuge	deception	pretence	trick

16

⊂A⊃	⊂B⊃	⊂C⊃	⊂D⊃	⊂E⊃
descendant	restorer	inheritor	replacement	follower

17

⊂A⊃	⊂B⊃	⊂C⊃	⊂D⊃	⊂E⊃
sluggish	inert	insipid	torpid	languid

Find The Missing Letters

Complete the sentence by identifying the missing letters. Write one letter into each of the large boxes below. After writing each letter, shade its corresponding element in the A-Z block beside it.

18 Despite vigorous efforts from virtually every advocate of religion, there has been a startling decline in interest in each further generation, and even an expansion of at□□□□m.

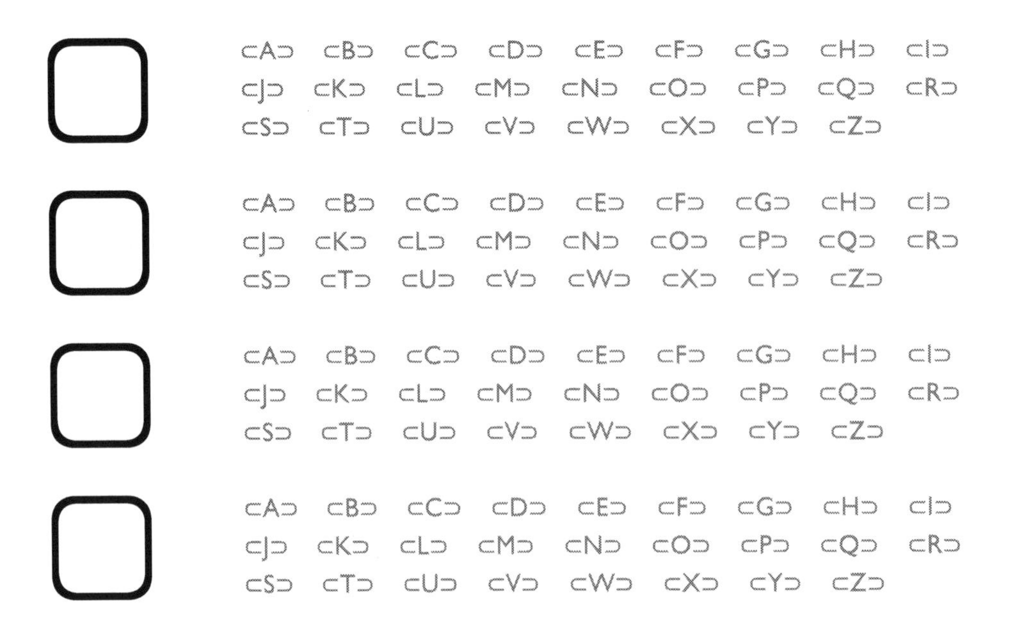

Similar relationships

Each sentence below states that one relationship is similar to another relationship. Choose the word, from options A to E, that completes the sentence best.

19

A	B	C	D	E
squeak	noisy	cool	sizzle	heat

Sonorous is to whistle as warm is to ______.

20

A	B	C	D	E
terminal	label	cellphone	wattage	power

Nib is to pen as battery is to ______.

21

A	B	C	D	E
float	sizzle	drift	shoal	flash

Dogs is to pack as fish is to ______.

Find The Missing Word

In each of the following pieces of text, one word is missing.
Complete it by choosing the one option A to E which fits best.

22

A	B	C	D	E
complement	complacent	compliment	complaisant	compliant

However much my mother asked for the leaking roof to be fixed, our landlord was quite ______, saying only that it would be dealt with in the fullness of time.

23

A	B	C	D	E
several	cereal	sequence	serial	coral

When the headmaster complained, "This is not the first time he has tossed his breakfast around mischievously; he is a ______ offender", he did not expect to be met with laughter.

Go to the next page 

24

A	B	C	D	E
Lets	Let's	Lets'	Let's'	Let

Please forgive my earlier rudeness. ______ let bygones be bygones, shall we? We must work together for the common good from now on.

25

A	B	C	D	E
adieu	do	ado	alas	advice

The train is just about to leave, so I must now bid you a fond ______ until we meet again.

26

A	B	C	D	E
prismatic	instantaneous	charismatic	spontaneous	cutaneous

Of course he persuaded the audience: he is one of the most ______ speakers in the world.

27

A	B	C	D	E
casement	storey	elevation	story	education

The teachers were delighted with the ______ that the newspaper produced, covering their tremendous examination success this year. All the hard work of pupils and teachers had paid off.

28

A	B	C	D	E
development	brevity	characters	descriptions	background

Thank you for telling your tale. However in future I would suggest you focus more on ______, since it did drag on for over an hour.

29

⊂A⊃	⊂B⊃	⊂C⊃	⊂D⊃	⊂E⊃
divergent	all together	distracted	altogether	distributed

The teachers did not want any children getting lost in the huge museum; they tried to keep them ______.

30

⊂A⊃	⊂B⊃	⊂C⊃	⊂D⊃	⊂E⊃
site	house	sight	home	cite

I am eager to come and visit the building ______ where the new school is in the process of being constructed.

This is the end of the training session.
Read the explanations at the back. In the box below, note any words you came across that were unfamiliar, together with a meaning or an example of usage. Practice using these words with adults.

Word	A short sentence *you* have created, using the word

Training Session 27

Matching Words

Identify which word is MOST SIMILAR in meaning to the word on the left. Each question has only one best answer. For each question shade your one chosen answer.

		A	B	C	D	E
1	**rural**	mountainous	steady	country	turning	folded
2	**consideration**	application	contemplation	attachment	adjacency	internalisation
3	**principle**	fancy	basis	headmaster	sovereign	subordinate
4	**reign**	regulation	rule	insist	drizzle	hook
5	**policy**	strategy	authority	security	arrest	guard
6	**revolution**	matrix	modification	cornering	improvement	overthrow
7	**scope**	withstand	extend	incorporate	miniaturise	range

Opposite Words

Identify which word is MOST OPPOSITE in meaning to the word on the left. Each question has only one best answer. For each question shade your one chosen answer.

		A	B	C	D	E
8	**quaint**	certain	fifth	uncountable	ancient	ordinary
9	**insane**	unwise	clean	crazy	slow	sound

Words That Do Not Match

Identify which of the 5 options A-E matches LEAST WELL in meaning to the word on the left. There is only one best answer. Shade your one chosen answer.

		A	B	C	D	E
10	**sanctuary**	refuge	haven	park	refuse	reserve
11	**soothing**	allaying	appeasing	comforting	sucking	mollifying

Odd One Out

Each group has four words which can have similar meanings, and one word which is different. Find the odd one out. Shade your one chosen answer.

	A	B	C	D	E
12	unimportant	triplicate	immaterial	trivial	trifling
13	poultry	petty	slight	paltry	insignificant

Go to the next page 

14

⊂A⊃	⊂B⊃	⊂C⊃	⊂D⊃	⊂E⊃
concise	message	brief	succinct	terse

15

⊂A⊃	⊂B⊃	⊂C⊃	⊂D⊃	⊂E⊃
loosen	relax	abate	slacken	abdicate

16

⊂A⊃	⊂B⊃	⊂C⊃	⊂D⊃	⊂E⊃
exceptional	singular	everyday	rare	infrequent

17

⊂A⊃	⊂B⊃	⊂C⊃	⊂D⊃	⊂E⊃
concurrent	electrical	simultaneous	contemporary	coexistent

Find The Missing Letters

Complete the sentence by identifying the missing letters. Write one letter into each of the large boxes below. After writing each letter, shade its corresponding element in the A-Z block beside it.

18 One small mistake was all it took to destroy the young lawyer's career. Being caught stealing from the law courts caused every one of his c□□□□ts to desert him, one by one.

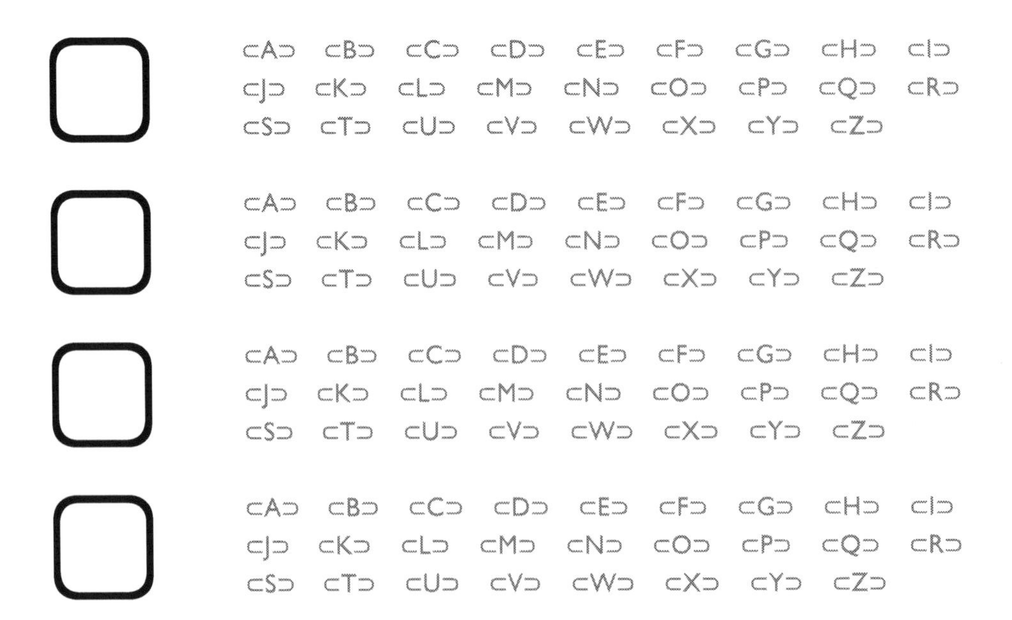

Similar relationships

Each sentence below states that one relationship is similar to another relationship. Choose the word, from options A to E, that completes the sentence best.

19

A	B	C	D	E
egg	scowl	brood	pie	sulk

Finches is to charm as chicks is to ______.

20

A	B	C	D	E
park	garden	repair	garage	petrol

Piggybank is to coins as car is to ______.

21

A	B	C	D	E
pounce	flock	stand	herd	gaze

Bee is to swarm as raccoon is to ______.

Find The Missing Word

In each of the following pieces of text, one word is missing.
Complete it by choosing the one option A to E which fits best.

22

A	B	C	D	E
molestation	anger	gymnastic	auspice	eccentric

While some people find his antics threatening, I think of him more as a harmless ______.

23

A	B	C	D	E
clamour	phase	cheering	face	faze

The sudden loud siren meant the game had moved into its final and most dramatic ______, with players now allowed to run across the lines that had previously served as barriers.

Go to the next page 

24

⊂A⊃	⊂B⊃	⊂C⊃	⊂D⊃	⊂E⊃
brought	born	bone	borne	brawn

When my father presented me for my birthday with the Giant Book of Hard Maths Sums, I wished I had never been ______.

25

⊂A⊃	⊂B⊃	⊂C⊃	⊂D⊃	⊂E⊃
patient	patient's	patients	patients'	patience

Few doctors advise their ______ to stop taking conventional heart medication and switch over entirely to homeopathic remedies.

26

⊂A⊃	⊂B⊃	⊂C⊃	⊂D⊃	⊂E⊃
elongation	impudence	pomposity	rapaciousness	invective

Victoria's circuit of her staff gave off such an air of ______ that they struggled to resist bursting into laughter.

27

⊂A⊃	⊂B⊃	⊂C⊃	⊂D⊃	⊂E⊃
deluded	derided	ridiculous	ridden	declined

I have no idea why he insists the waiter stole his wallet. We have proved to him that this is not the case but he remains ______.

28

⊂A⊃	⊂B⊃	⊂C⊃	⊂D⊃	⊂E⊃
joy	delight	attenuated	blissful	nocturnal

I spent a ______ evening at the spa, having my skin rejuvenated and the bags under my eyes smoothed away.

29

A	B	C	D	E
obedience	camaraderie	defiance	artistry	obeisance

As a sign of ______, he painted over the insignia of the new ruler in thick red paint.

30

A	B	C	D	E
attack	rude	reject	comply	box

Much as I would enjoy the opportunity to ______ your impertinent ears one more time, I think I will pass up the offer on this occasion.

This is the end of the training session.

Read the explanations at the back. In the box below, note any words you came across that were unfamiliar, together with a meaning or an example of usage. Practice using these words with adults.

Word	A short sentence *you* have created, using the word

Training Session 28

Matching Words

Identify which word is MOST SIMILAR in meaning to the word on the left. Each question has only one best answer. For each question shade your one chosen answer.

		A	B	C	D	E
1	**hilarious**	illegal	instinctive	thieving	critical	amusing
2	**florid**	hydrated	increased	repulsed	handy	flamboyant
3	**slander**	competition	misrepresent	tilt	augment	slim
4	**prosperous**	exhausting	ridiculous	hopeful	fearful	successful
5	**ornate**	elaborate	explain	circular	roundabout	alternative
6	**incline**	beg	shiver	request	preach	favour
7	**pious**	tasty	spiritual	rounded	laborious	enormous

Opposite Words

Identify which word is MOST OPPOSITE in meaning to the word on the left. Each question has only one best answer. For each question shade your one chosen answer.

		A	B	C	D	E
8	**contrary**	rejecting	region	hostile	hurtful	agreeable
9	**jovial**	morose	breakable	jocular	smooth	jolly

Words That Do Not Match

Identify which of the 5 options A-E matches LEAST WELL in meaning to the word on the left. There is only one best answer. Shade your one chosen answer.

		A	B	C	D	E
10	**homogeneous**	unvarying	identical	irregular	alike	matching
11	**objective**	destination	fair	complain	aim	neutral

Odd One Out

Each group has four words which can have similar meanings, and one word which is different. Find the odd one out. Shade your one chosen answer.

	A	B	C	D	E
12	holed	riddled	previous	porous	pervious
13	explosive	bombastic	grandiose	pompous	pretentious

Go to the next page 

14 ⊂A⊃ narrow ⊂B⊃ contract ⊂C⊃ promise ⊂D⊃ shrink ⊂E⊃ reduce

15 ⊂A⊃ baffling ⊂B⊃ illusive ⊂C⊃ shifty ⊂D⊃ elusive ⊂E⊃ slippery

16 ⊂A⊃ withdraw ⊂B⊃ backtrack ⊂C⊃ retire ⊂D⊃ inflict ⊂E⊃ retreat

17 ⊂A⊃ reform ⊂B⊃ mollify ⊂C⊃ change ⊂D⊃ adjust ⊂E⊃ modify

Find The Missing Letters

Complete the sentence by identifying the missing letters. Write one letter into each of the large boxes below. After writing each letter, shade its corresponding element in the A-Z block beside it.

18 Twenty horses at full gallop later, the previously clear water of the pond was now hopelessly mu□□□□d, leaving little chance to spear individual fish by sight, as we had originally hoped.

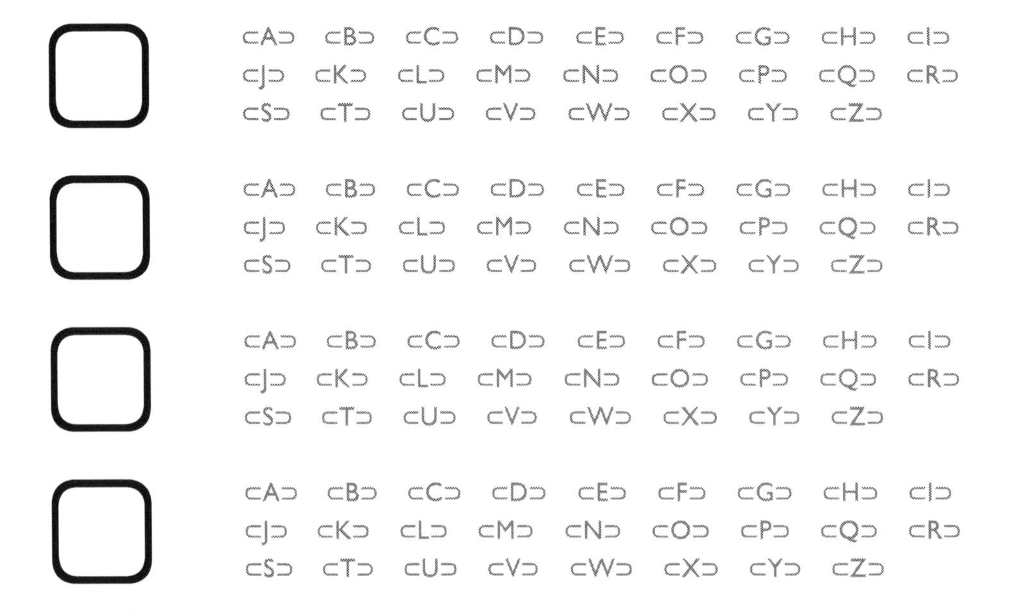

Similar relationships

Each sentence below states that one relationship is similar to another relationship. Choose the word, from options A to E, that completes the sentence best.

19

A	B	C	D	E
legal	furtive	decisive	wallet	theft

Athletics is to sporty as thieving is to _______.

20

A	B	C	D	E
network	conclave	clove	brief	nest

Bee is to hive as hornet is to _______.

21

A	B	C	D	E
piece	capture	game	spurn	king

Baseball is to sport as chess is to _______.

Find The Missing Word

In each of the following pieces of text, one word is missing.
Complete it by choosing the one option A to E which fits best.

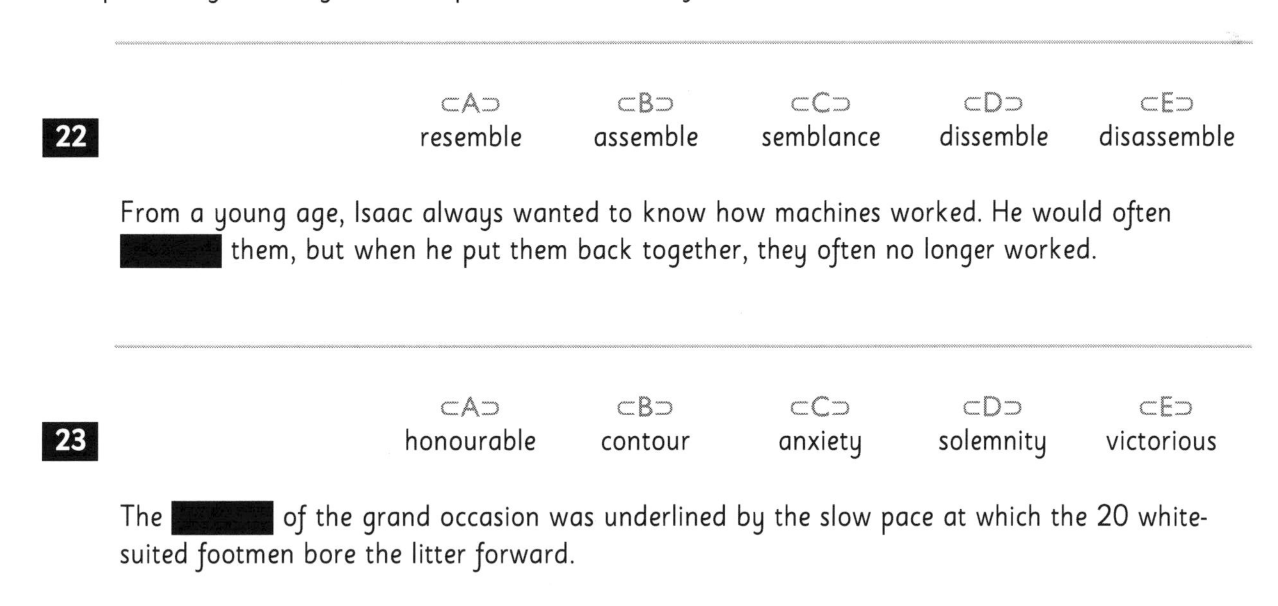

22

A	B	C	D	E
resemble	assemble	semblance	dissemble	disassemble

From a young age, Isaac always wanted to know how machines worked. He would often _______ them, but when he put them back together, they often no longer worked.

23

A	B	C	D	E
honourable	contour	anxiety	solemnity	victorious

The _______ of the grand occasion was underlined by the slow pace at which the 20 white-suited footmen bore the litter forward.

Go to the next page ➡

24

⊂A⊃	⊂B⊃	⊂C⊃	⊂D⊃	⊂E⊃
serendipitously	conveniently	incomparably	likewise	until

The drama teacher distributed the dresses amongst the girls according to their preference for colours; ________ she distributed the T-shirts amongst the boys according to their preferences.

25

⊂A⊃	⊂B⊃	⊂C⊃	⊂D⊃	⊂E⊃
aberrant	starving	abstruse	abhorrent	delicious

However short of money we were, however much we had to scrimp and save for every morsel, even still the mere suggestion that I should steal food was ________ to me.

26

⊂A⊃	⊂B⊃	⊂C⊃	⊂D⊃	⊂E⊃
sighed	sight	side	site	cite

It is difficult for me to undo my shirt buttons at my age because my ________ is not what it was.

27

⊂A⊃	⊂B⊃	⊂C⊃	⊂D⊃	⊂E⊃
countrys	country's	countries	countrie's	countries'

Resplendent in their many-coloured robes, the twenty ________ representatives glided to the conference room and gradually took their seats in a dignified manner.

28

⊂A⊃	⊂B⊃	⊂C⊃	⊂D⊃	⊂E⊃
adjuvant	immaculate	turbid	rotatory	scientist

Swilling the glass flask around a few times, she looked closely at the ________ mixture, and was surprised to see a pair of eyes looking back at her through the cloud of debris.

29

A	B	C	D	E
noteworthy	expensive	elongated	convincing	forgettable

Of all the paintings in the exhibition, the most ██████ is the one depicting the woman reclining in the white T shirt and black shorts: the quizzical tilt of her head drew much discussion.

30

A	B	C	D	E
practical	proxy	practise	proactive	practice

You are right that I have been very lucky in my exams. However, the strange thing is that the more I ██████, the luckier I get. Can you think why?

This is the end of the training session.
Read the explanations at the back. In the box below, note any words you came across that were unfamiliar, together with a meaning or an example of usage. Practice using these words with adults.

Word	A short sentence *you* have created, using the word

Training Session 29

Matching Words

Identify which word is MOST SIMILAR in meaning to the word on the left. Each question has only one best answer. For each question shade your one chosen answer.

		A	B	C	D	E
1	**adore**	delay	entrance	serious	commotion	idolize
2	**recover**	remember	recuperate	explore	overgrow	confuse
3	**taciturn**	spinning	replying	reticent	garrulous	welcoming
4	**receptive**	responsive	captured	doorman	exclusion	recognition
5	**role**	nutrition	responsibility	bread	tumble	overturning
6	**umbrage**	resentment	shadowing	ferocity	youthfulness	shelter
7	**analogy**	prehistory	asymmetry	infamy	biology	parallelism

Opposite Words

Identify which word is MOST OPPOSITE in meaning to the word on the left. Each question has only one best answer. For each question shade your one chosen answer.

		A	B	C	D	E
8	**restrain**	harness	re-educate	imprison	assist	confuse
9	**heed**	thought	vigilance	observe	inaction	ignore

Words That Do Not Match

Identify which of the 5 options A-E matches LEAST WELL in meaning to the word on the left. There is only one best answer. Shade your one chosen answer.

		A	B	C	D	E
10	**provoke**	instigate	irk	initiate	cancel	annoy
11	**malady**	ailment	sickness	harmony	illness	affliction

Odd One Out

Each group has four words which can have similar meanings, and one word which is different. Find the odd one out. Shade your one chosen answer.

	A	B	C	D	E
12	disrepute	ignominy	disgrace	shame	disrepair
13	lesson	wane	ebb	lessen	decline

Go to the next page 

	A	B	C	D	E
14	servile	lavish	menial	slavish	cringing
15	serious	sober	sedate	certain	subdued
16	opening	interval	gap	gulf	ocean
17	option	extra	choice	selection	election

Find The Missing Letters

Complete the sentence by identifying the missing letters. Write one letter into each of the large boxes below. After writing each letter, shade its corresponding element in the A-Z block beside it.

18 It was difficult to explain to the investors what we had in mind, because they just could not con□□□□e of the idea of a gigantic computer program that searched the internet and stored the results so anyone could find information quickly.

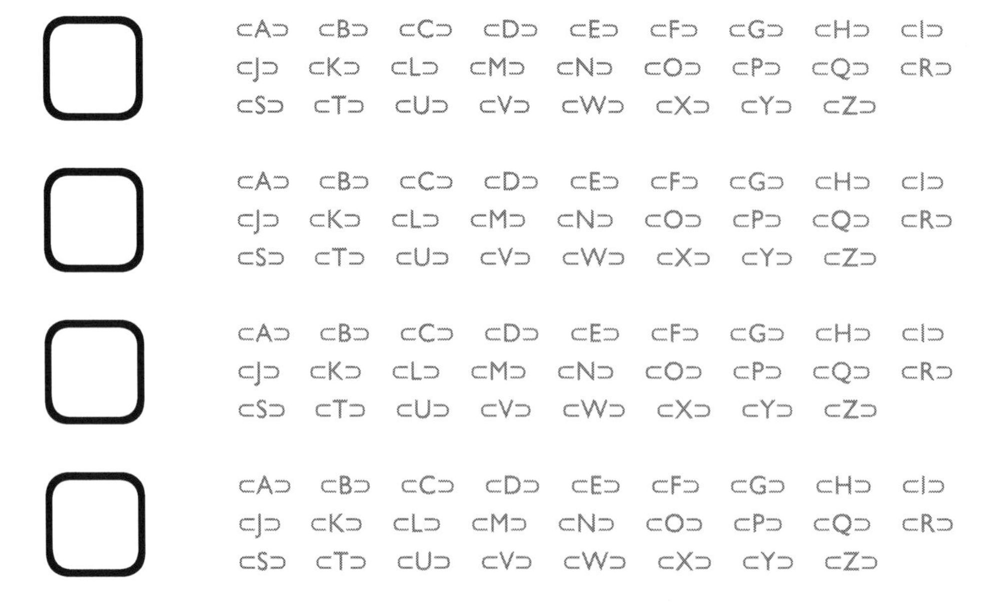

Similar relationships

Each sentence below states that one relationship is similar to another relationship. Choose the word, from options A to E, that completes the sentence best.

19

A	B	C	D	E
slant	herd	sty	house	pack

Jays is to band as hounds is to ______.

20

A	B	C	D	E
Italy	Russia	China	Germany	Ireland

Noodles is to Japan as spaghetti is to ______.

21

A	B	C	D	E
disorder	repository	army	bite	tirade

Buffalo is to herd as ants is to ______.

Find The Missing Word

In each of the following pieces of text, one word is missing.
Complete it by choosing the one option A to E which fits best.

22

A	B	C	D	E
campanologist	colonist	cryptographer	cosmologist	chauvinist

Insisting that only Britons should be allowed to write in the magazine, Derek revealed he was still just as much a ______ as ever.

23

A	B	C	D	E
ozone	climactic	climatic	impossible	deforestation

In recent years evidence has accumulated that there are subtle, progressive ______ changes worldwide, that point to worsening desertification and rising sea levels in the decades to come.

Go to the next page ➡

24

A	B	C	D	E
fractionation	fanclub	fictionalisation	fanaticism	acceptance

After decades of government leaders repeatedly insulting and mistreating this minority tribe, there was a growing tendency to ______ amongst its younger members.

25

A	B	C	D	E
cob	crumb	crab	cop	crib

My plan to cheat on the exams by taking in a ______ sheet was foiled by the eagle-eyed invigilator.

26

A	B	C	D	E
decadent	obligatory	decade	respected	misspent

Sadly, he ______ his youth, focusing on wine and dice, rather than on building a portfolio of transferrable skills and qualifications.

27

A	B	C	D	E
cores	course	coarse	curse	cruise

Her lightweight dress was little comfort to her as she waited in the snowscape for rescue. How she regretted discarding the ______, unfashionable overcoat in her ill-fated preparation for the party.

28

A	B	C	D	E
scent	ascent	assess	assent	sent

Unfortunately, because driving rain and sleet had now arrived, finding our way down from the mountain peak was not easier than our ______ of it in good weather the day before.

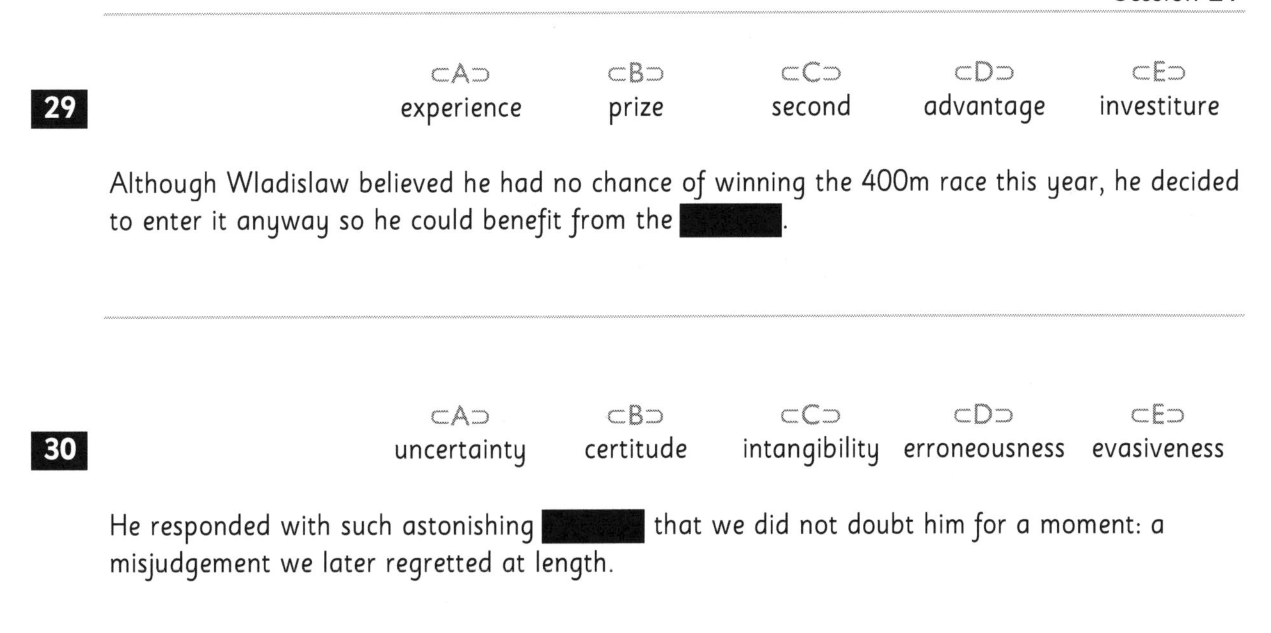

29

⊂A⊃	⊂B⊃	⊂C⊃	⊂D⊃	⊂E⊃
experience	prize	second	advantage	investiture

Although Wladislaw believed he had no chance of winning the 400m race this year, he decided to enter it anyway so he could benefit from the ______.

30

⊂A⊃	⊂B⊃	⊂C⊃	⊂D⊃	⊂E⊃
uncertainty	certitude	intangibility	erroneousness	evasiveness

He responded with such astonishing ______ that we did not doubt him for a moment: a misjudgement we later regretted at length.

This is the end of the training session.
Read the explanations at the back. In the box below, note any words you came across that were unfamiliar, together with a meaning or an example of usage. Practice using these words with adults.

Word	A short sentence *you* have created, using the word

Training Session 30

Matching Words

Identify which word is MOST SIMILAR in meaning to the word on the left. Each question has only one best answer. For each question shade your one chosen answer.

		A	B	C	D	E
1	**integral**	essential	advertised	vulgar	educated	elliptical
2	**reproach**	scold	approximate	overcook	near	enclose
3	**contrite**	manage	re-establish	rewrite	correct	sorry
4	**nauseous**	disobedient	queasy	boisterous	unlucky	mismatched
5	**sombre**	rinse	downcast	headdress	broadcast	hat
6	**sacrifice**	courage	person	slaughter	precipice	generosity
7	**resigned**	elected	continued	accepting	repeated	replaced

Opposite Words

Identify which word is MOST OPPOSITE in meaning to the word on the left. Each question has only one best answer. For each question shade your one chosen answer.

		A	B	C	D	E
8	**conclusion**	termination	escape	start	explanation	decision
9	**compelling**	tiring	forced	retiring	convincing	dull

Words That Do Not Match

Identify which of the 5 options A-E matches LEAST WELL in meaning to the word on the left. There is only one best answer. Shade your one chosen answer.

		A	B	C	D	E
10	**simulate**	initiate	pretend	affect	counterfeit	imitate
11	**distress**	separation	sorrow	anguish	need	agony

Odd One Out

Each group has four words which can have similar meanings, and one word which is different. Find the odd one out. Shade your one chosen answer.

	A	B	C	D	E
12	verbose	adjective	redundant	repetitive	superfluous
13	precarious	unsteady	unsure	uncertain	uniform

Go to the next page 

	(A)	(B)	(C)	(D)	(E)
14	babbling	talkative	verbose	sentimental	garrulous
15	sure	intrepid	confident	assured	confidant
16	grow	swell	increase	flicker	thrive
17	strange	bazaar	peculiar	eccentric	bizarre

Find The Missing Letters

Complete the sentence by identifying the missing letters. Write one letter into each of the large boxes below. After writing each letter, shade its corresponding element in the A-Z block beside it.

18 As the thirteen-day-old phone bounced off the ceiling and fell back into her hand totally blank and lifeless, Geraldine recalled with glee that the no-questions-asked g□□□□ntee lasted for two weeks. She could rescue the situation if she acted immediately.

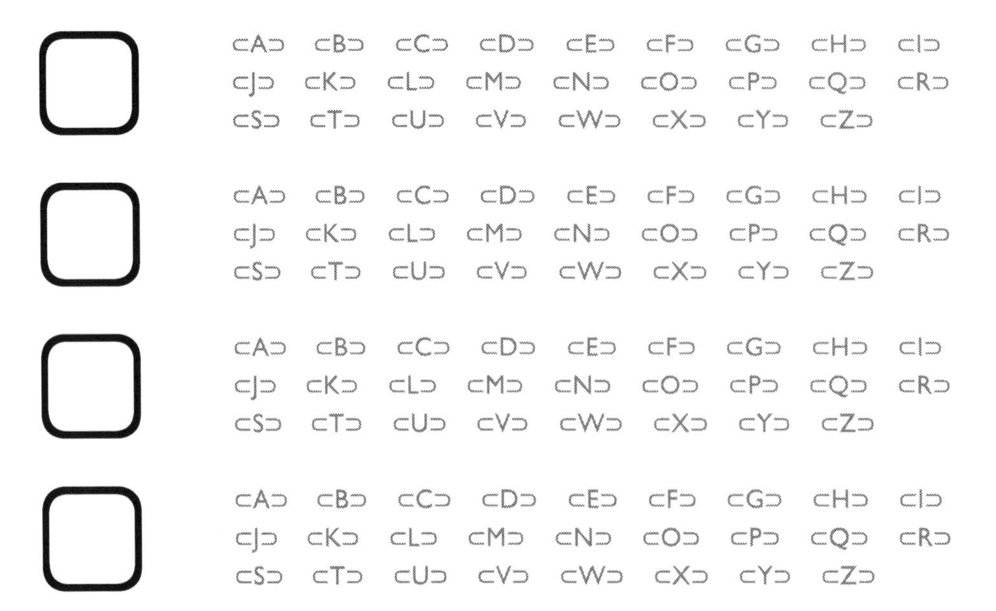

Similar relationships

Each sentence below states that one relationship is similar to another relationship. Choose the word, from options A to E, that completes the sentence best.

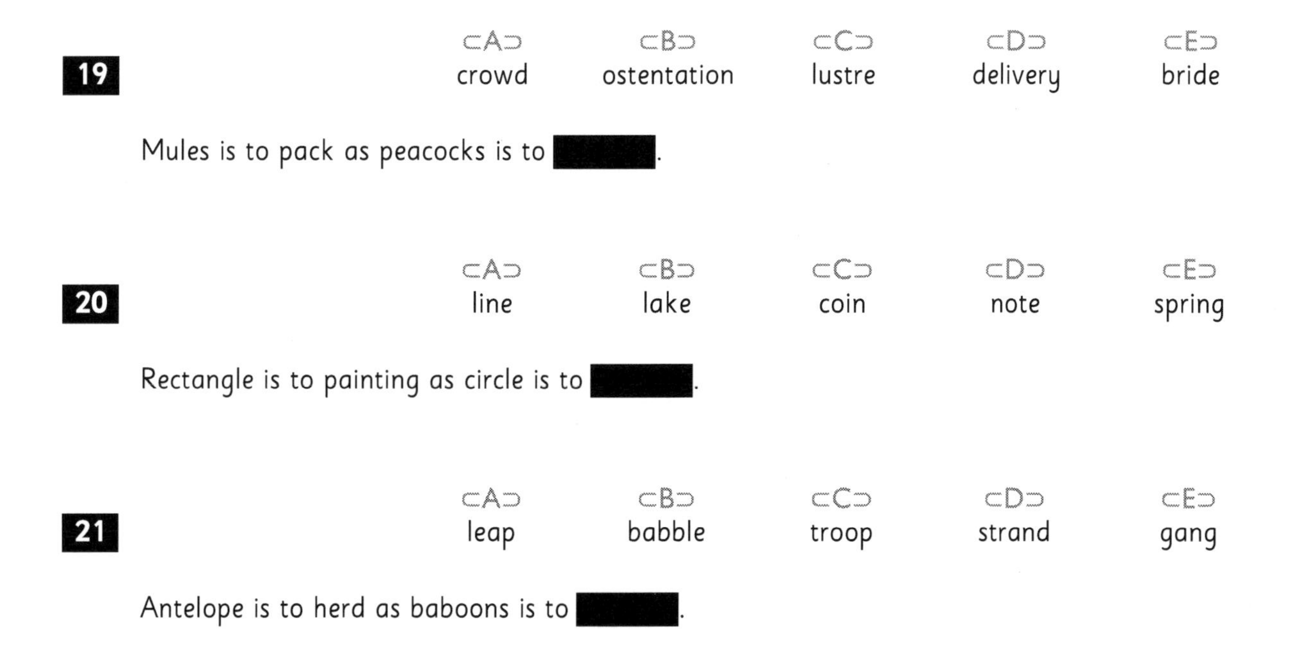

19

A	B	C	D	E
crowd	ostentation	lustre	delivery	bride

Mules is to pack as peacocks is to ______.

20

A	B	C	D	E
line	lake	coin	note	spring

Rectangle is to painting as circle is to ______.

21

A	B	C	D	E
leap	babble	troop	strand	gang

Antelope is to herd as baboons is to ______.

Find The Missing Word

In each of the following pieces of text, one word is missing.
Complete it by choosing the one option A to E which fits best.

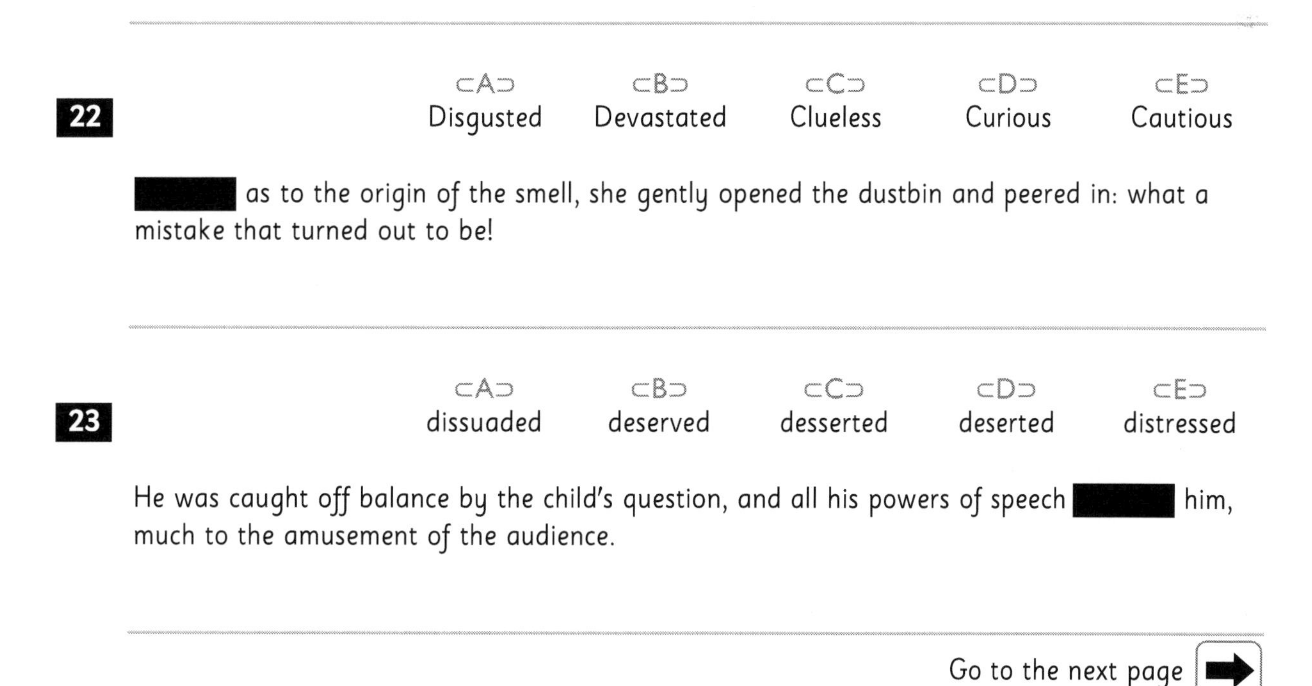

22

A	B	C	D	E
Disgusted	Devastated	Clueless	Curious	Cautious

______ as to the origin of the smell, she gently opened the dustbin and peered in: what a mistake that turned out to be!

23

A	B	C	D	E
dissuaded	deserved	desserted	deserted	distressed

He was caught off balance by the child's question, and all his powers of speech ______ him, much to the amusement of the audience.

Go to the next page

24

⊂A⊃	⊂B⊃	⊂C⊃	⊂D⊃	⊂E⊃
aspect	room	expect	accept	except

When you say you are unhappy with your stay in our hotel, which ______ of it would you say was the most troubling?

25

⊂A⊃	⊂B⊃	⊂C⊃	⊂D⊃	⊂E⊃
year	years	year'	year's	years'

Two ______ work very nearly went down the drain when a computer virus stormed into life on our system and even destroyed our backup copies.

26

⊂A⊃	⊂B⊃	⊂C⊃	⊂D⊃	⊂E⊃
chronicle	circumstance	antediluvian	cistern	instantaneous

In this particular ______ we will allow you to enter the auditorium late, but do not assume that this is a precedent for the future.

27

⊂A⊃	⊂B⊃	⊂C⊃	⊂D⊃	⊂E⊃
stratify	levitate	increase	underline	denote

In this formula, the letter y will ______ the number 4.

28

⊂A⊃	⊂B⊃	⊂C⊃	⊂D⊃	⊂E⊃
lice	lose	untied	unlocked	loose

I will set you ______ if you promise that you will stop harassing us. We are only trying to eat our picnic and you have been very destructive for no reason. Alternatively, if you prefer to remain tied to this tree, please let me know.

29

A	B	C	D	E
downfall	nemesis	assistant	comrade	genesis

Finally cornered in a quarry and with no means of escape, Nico warily eyed his ______ who was just coming into sight in the distance. The relentless policeman would finally have his day.

30

A	B	C	D	E
its	it	it's	its'	it's'

Driven into a frenzy by the itching, the dog rolled over onto ______ side and began a ferocious wriggling dance in the dry earth.

This is the end of the training session.

Read the explanations at the back. In the box below, note any words you came across that were unfamiliar, together with a meaning or an example of usage. Practice using these words with adults.

Word	A short sentence *you* have created, using the word

Training Session 31

Matching Words

Identify which word is MOST SIMILAR in meaning to the word on the left. Each question has only one best answer. For each question shade your one chosen answer.

		A	B	C	D	E
1	**forebear**	receive	relinquish	carry	ancestor	withstand
2	**forsake**	abandon	respect	purpose	clearing	agony
3	**steadfast**	dependable	replacement	tightened	rushed	elongated
4	**contemplate**	original	undersurface	replicate	stare	flatten
5	**stubborn**	kind-hearted	awakened	awkward	signal	lyrical
6	**retain**	castle	relearn	preserve	homecoming	inscribed
7	**aesthetic**	painless	fragrant	beautiful	personal	connected

Opposite Words

Identify which word is MOST OPPOSITE in meaning to the word on the left. Each question has only one best answer. For each question shade your one chosen answer.

		A	B	C	D	E
8	**obvious**	clear	manifest	noticeable	plain	subtle
9	**sturdy**	ignore	waste	engross	flimsy	read

Words That Do Not Match

Identify which of the 5 options A-E matches LEAST WELL in meaning to the word on the left. There is only one best answer. Shade your one chosen answer.

		A	B	C	D	E
10	**hostile**	aggressive	averse	altitude	warlike	militant
11	**adversary**	foe	challenger	nemesis	poetry	rival

Odd One Out

Each group has four words which can have similar meanings, and one word which is different. Find the odd one out. Shade your one chosen answer.

	A	B	C	D	E
12	nuance	underground	subtlety	sophistication	delicacy
13	following	next	ensuing	suing	later

Go to the next page 

	⊂A⊃	⊂B⊃	⊂C⊃	⊂D⊃	⊂E⊃
14	constrict	overwork	constrain	inhibit	limit
15	deserter	traitor	betrayer	cower	renegade
16	kindly	benign	perturbed	benevolent	gentle
17	speedy	nimble	fleet	impulse	swift

Find The Missing Letters

Complete the sentence by identifying the missing letters. Write one letter into each of the large boxes below. After writing each letter, shade its corresponding element in the A-Z block beside it.

18 How can you leave those children to starve while you stuff yourself to the gills with unneccessary excess pudding? Have you no con□□□□nce at all?

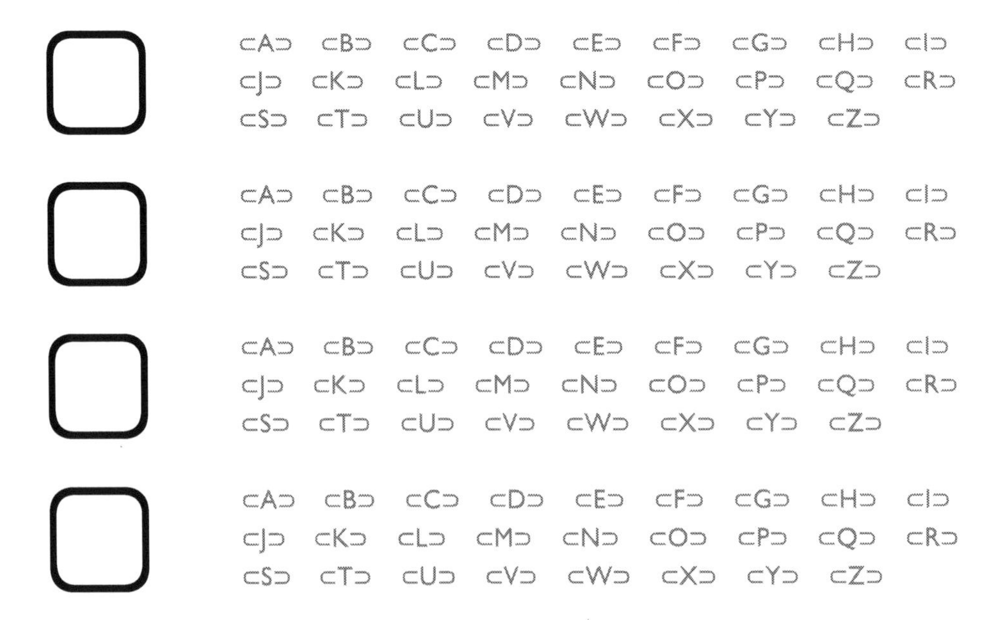

Similar relationships

Each sentence below states that one relationship is similar to another relationship. Choose the word, *from* options A to E, that completes the sentence best.

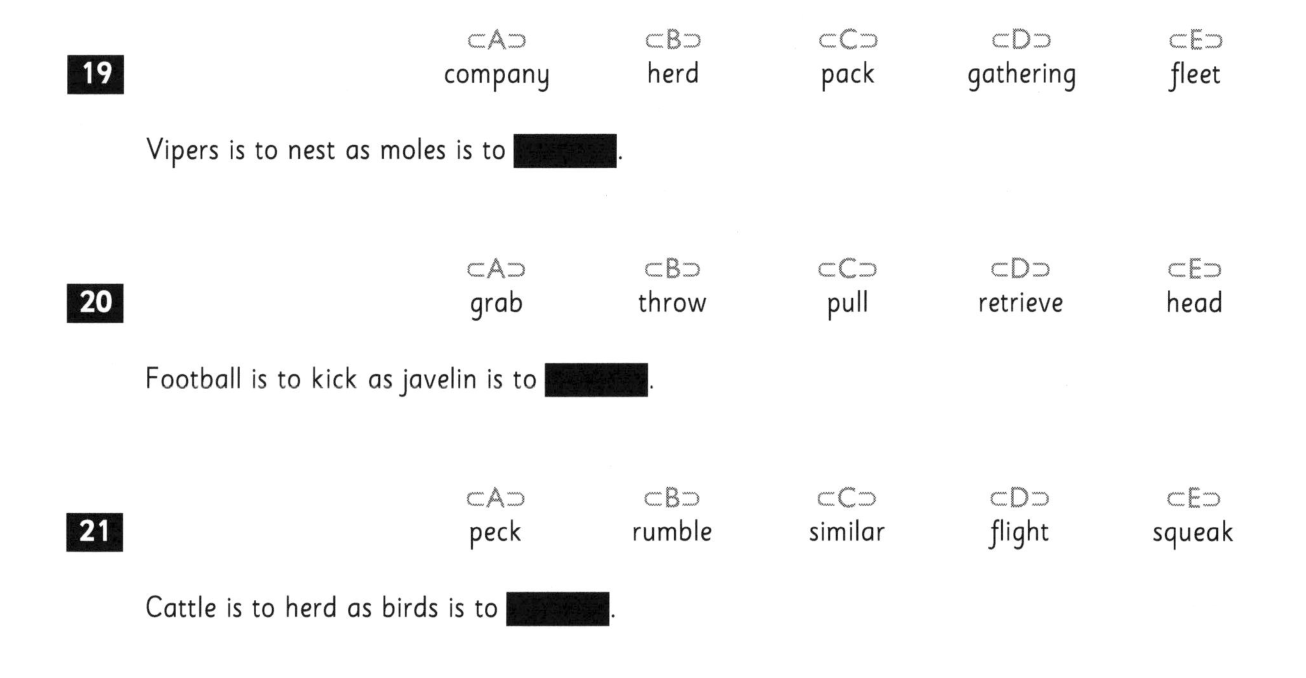

19

A	B	C	D	E
company	herd	pack	gathering	fleet

Vipers is to nest as moles is to ______.

20

A	B	C	D	E
grab	throw	pull	retrieve	head

Football is to kick as javelin is to ______.

21

A	B	C	D	E
peck	rumble	similar	flight	squeak

Cattle is to herd as birds is to ______.

Find The Missing Word

In each *of* the *following* pieces *of* text, one word is missing.
Complete it by choosing the one option A to E which *fits* best.

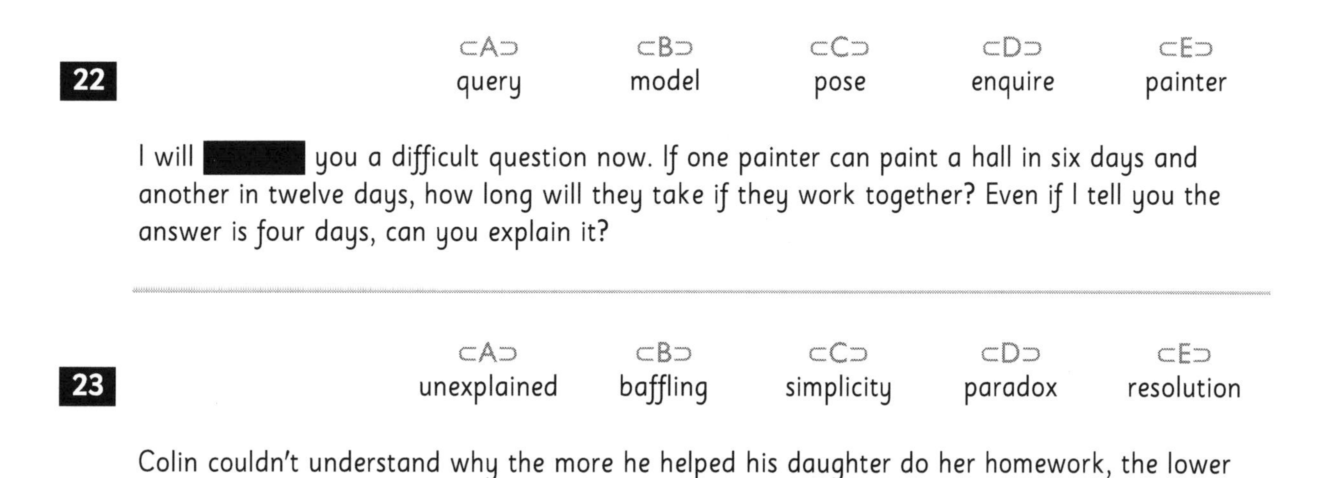

22

A	B	C	D	E
query	model	pose	enquire	painter

I will ______ you a difficult question now. If one painter can paint a hall in six days and another in twelve days, how long will they take if they work together? Even if I tell you the answer is four days, can you explain it?

23

A	B	C	D	E
unexplained	baffling	simplicity	paradox	resolution

Colin couldn't understand why the more he helped his daughter do her homework, the lower the marks she obtained in her exams. To him it was a ______, but the explanation is simple: when he did the homework, it was he who was learning and not she.

Go to the next page 

24

⊂A⊃	⊂B⊃	⊂C⊃	⊂D⊃	⊂E⊃
general	including	overall	without	sharpened

"Yes, ladies and gentlemen, this is an absolute bargain," droned the tedious presenter faking interest in another tatty set of carving knives. "And the price is only £19.95 ______ VAT, postage and packing, so there is nothing more to pay."

25

⊂A⊃	⊂B⊃	⊂C⊃	⊂D⊃	⊂E⊃
insure	encasing	examine	protection	ensure

That is a very expensive watch I see on your wrist. I do suggest you ______ it because it will be very attractive to thieves.

26

⊂A⊃	⊂B⊃	⊂C⊃	⊂D⊃	⊂E⊃
squinting	majesty	glory	musical	resplendent

Ria had often caught Ian's eye in the past, but at tonight's ball she was truly ______ in an elegant green gown studded with sequins and gold embroidery.

27

⊂A⊃	⊂B⊃	⊂C⊃	⊂D⊃	⊂E⊃
party	restaurant	hole	hotel	aviary

A continuous hum from thousands of fluttering wings filled the air as we descended into the centre of the giant ______, surrounded by what seemed like millions of birds of all shapes, sizes and colours.

28

⊂A⊃	⊂B⊃	⊂C⊃	⊂D⊃	⊂E⊃
villagers	protester	foliage	mountain	leaf

I would have enjoyed the trip to Borneo more if I didn't have to spend half my time pushing back the ______ that blocked my every step, but I suppose it is partly my fault for choosing an uninhabited area with no roads or paths.

29

⊂A⊃	⊂B⊃	⊂C⊃	⊂D⊃	⊂E⊃
impressive	pickpocket	notable	innocent	inconspicuous

As the policeman slowly surveyed the passengers on the bus that he had stopped, Malcolm tried to make himself ______, dumping his catch of stolen wallets into the shopping bag of the woman beside him.

30

⊂A⊃	⊂B⊃	⊂C⊃	⊂D⊃	⊂E⊃
misfortune	guilty	pretty	auspicious	innocent

One month later, sitting in the dock at the courthouse, Malcolm rued the day he tipped the evidence into the shopping bag of the policeman's mother. As the verdict was about to be delivered, the expressions on the jury's faces were unfortunately not ______.

This is the end of the training session.
Read the explanations at the back. In the box below, note any words you came across that were unfamiliar, together with a meaning or an example of usage. Practice using these words with adults.

Word	A short sentence *you* have created, using the word

Training Session 32

Matching Words

Identify which word is MOST SIMILAR in meaning to the word on the left. Each question has only one best answer. For each question shade your one chosen answer.

		A	B	C	D	E
1	**gratuitous**	violent	thankful	schooled	chopped	unwarranted
2	**precipitate**	trigger	derange	oscillate	accommodate	concern
3	**respite**	revenge	nevertheless	viciousness	though	hiatus
4	**authentic**	genuine	gorgeous	painted	remembered	resolute
5	**bilious**	quivering	nauseated	wobbling	expensive	naughty
6	**bemuse**	entertain	giggle	regulate	confuse	recommend
7	**respond**	underwater	second	recognise	reply	invoke

Opposite Words

Identify which word is MOST OPPOSITE in meaning to the word on the left. Each question has only one best answer. For each question shade your one chosen answer.

		A	B	C	D	E
8	**marred**	dieted	divorced	followed	perfected	barred
9	**transmit**	build	broadcast	receive	jettison	emit

Words That Do Not Match

Identify which of the 5 options A-E matches LEAST WELL in meaning to the word on the left. There is only one best answer. Shade your one chosen answer.

		A	B	C	D	E
10	**foster**	cultivated	encourage	strengthen	nurture	support
11	**mature**	grow	ripe	grown	sensible	fertiliser

Odd One Out

Each group has four words which can have similar meanings, and one word which is different. Find the odd one out. Shade your one chosen answer.

	A	B	C	D	E
12	surplus	maintain	bear	carry	sustain
13	wrestle	grapple	succumb	battle	contend

Go to the next page 

14

⊂A⊃	⊂B⊃	⊂C⊃	⊂D⊃	⊂E⊃
coy	diffident	bashful	shy	different

15

⊂A⊃	⊂B⊃	⊂C⊃	⊂D⊃	⊂E⊃
avocado	champion	proponent	advocate	backer

16

⊂A⊃	⊂B⊃	⊂C⊃	⊂D⊃	⊂E⊃
mindful	aware	tented	attentive	watchful

17

⊂A⊃	⊂B⊃	⊂C⊃	⊂D⊃	⊂E⊃
loath	averse	reticent	reluctant	hesitant

Find The Missing Letters

Complete the sentence by identifying the missing letters. Write one letter into each of the large boxes below. After writing each letter, shade its corresponding element in the A-Z block beside it.

18 After rough treatment by the villagers who captured me as I sneaked into their encampment, I was greatly relieved to find that their c☐☐☐f was a calm, gentle and civilised man.

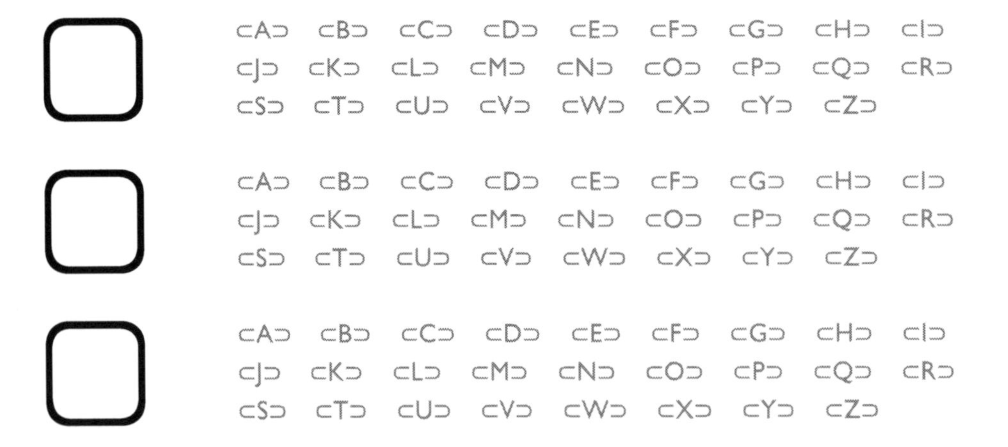

Similar relationships

Each sentence below states that one relationship is similar to another relationship. Choose the word, from options A to E, that completes the sentence best.

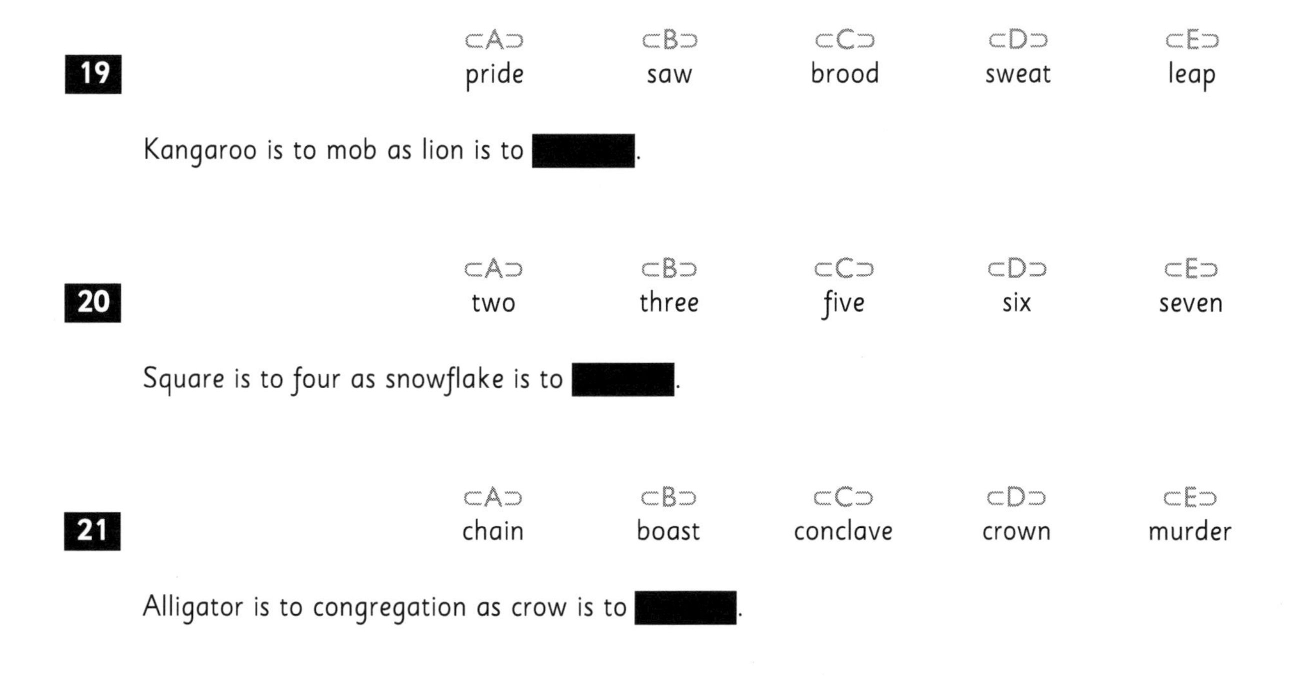

19

A	B	C	D	E
pride	saw	brood	sweat	leap

Kangaroo is to mob as lion is to ______.

20

A	B	C	D	E
two	three	five	six	seven

Square is to four as snowflake is to ______.

21

A	B	C	D	E
chain	boast	conclave	crown	murder

Alligator is to congregation as crow is to ______.

Find The Missing Word

In each of the following pieces of text, one word is missing.
Complete it by choosing the one option A to E which fits best.

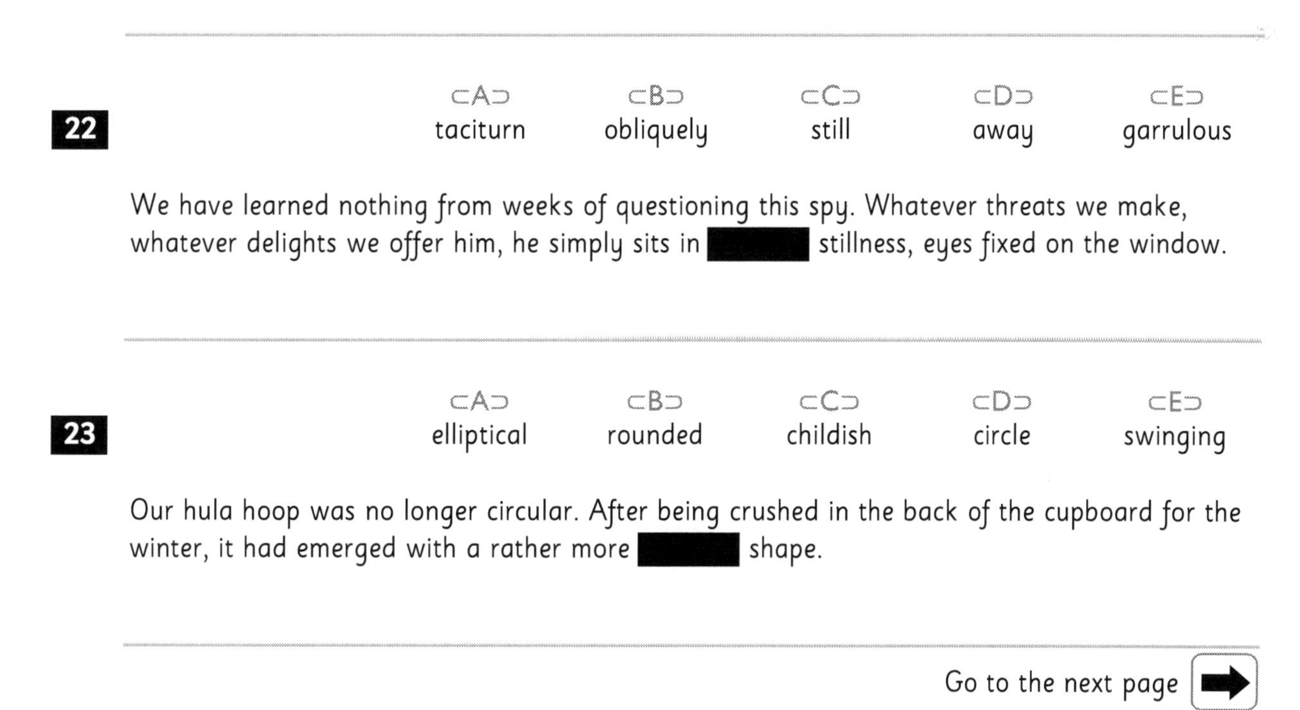

22

A	B	C	D	E
taciturn	obliquely	still	away	garrulous

We have learned nothing from weeks of questioning this spy. Whatever threats we make, whatever delights we offer him, he simply sits in ______ stillness, eyes fixed on the window.

23

A	B	C	D	E
elliptical	rounded	childish	circle	swinging

Our hula hoop was no longer circular. After being crushed in the back of the cupboard for the winter, it had emerged with a rather more ______ shape.

Go to the next page ➡

24

⊂A⊃	⊂B⊃	⊂C⊃	⊂D⊃	⊂E⊃
mystery	confusion	homonym	difficult	trouble

Box is a classic ______. It can mean to play the sport of boxing, using gloves to strike your opponent, or can mean a container typically with a rectangular outline. Both words are spelt and pronounced identically.

25

⊂A⊃	⊂B⊃	⊂C⊃	⊂D⊃	⊂E⊃
transmutation	neutralisation	levitation	veto	abolish

The law doubling the salary of members of parliament was passed with unsurprising enthusiasm by those very same individuals, but fortunately for the national purse the Queen applied her power of ______ to prevent it coming into force.

26

⊂A⊃	⊂B⊃	⊂C⊃	⊂D⊃	⊂E⊃
begging	rudely	desperately	ostensibly	seeming

Josey made her way back into the museum, ______ to retrieve her handbag which she had left in one of the viewing rooms, but in reality to wedge open the side exit door. "It's all or nothing tonight," she said to herself on the way out, muscles already tensed with anticipation.

27

⊂A⊃	⊂B⊃	⊂C⊃	⊂D⊃	⊂E⊃
unmask	report	repast	calculation	conflagration

Even though we only gave her a couple of hours' notice, she came up with a luxurious ______ for our entire group of hungry managers. She is truly a domestic goddess as well as being our Chief Financial Officer.

28

⊂A⊃	⊂B⊃	⊂C⊃	⊂D⊃	⊂E⊃
devotion	rapture	pawn	capture	happy

While I had always enjoyed winning chess contests, the day I was lucky enough to win against a local grandmaster distracted by other games he was playing simultaneously, I was in ______. It was the happiest day of my life.

29

A	B	C	D	E
surely	curly	burly	surly	early

Although he explained his reason for lateness, his teacher was ______, showing no interest or flexibility. He would be penalised, and there was no evading it.

30

A	B	C	D	E
pulled	taut	pulling	taught	tension

Hugo enjoyed the short story about the boy who ran away from home and endured many adventures before being reunited with his parents. It was a well-planned plot and the writing was ______, making for an enjoyable experience.

This is the end of the training session.

Read the explanations at the back. In the box below, note any words you came across that were unfamiliar, together with a meaning or an example of usage. Practice using these words with adults.

Word	A short sentence *you* have created, using the word

Training Session 33

Matching Words

Identify which word is MOST SIMILAR in meaning to the word on the left. Each question has only one best answer. For each question shade your one chosen answer.

		A	B	C	D	E
1	**purpose**	turtle	dolphin	objective	guesswork	hesitation
2	**avaricious**	greedy	amiable	birdlike	juicy	delicious
3	**exalt**	leave	rejoice	mutilate	personalise	praise
4	**trepidation**	entrapment	rejection	removal	apprehension	property
5	**singular**	controversial	striking	operator	co-operative	message
6	**controversy**	library	debate	aftermath	wilderness	ownership
7	**prescribe**	engrave	order	copy	calligrapher	forbid

Opposite Words

Identify which word is MOST OPPOSITE in meaning to the word on the left. Each question has only one best answer. For each question shade your one chosen answer.

		A	B	C	D	E
8	**pacifying**	infuriating	exercising	soothing	covering	placating
9	**austerity**	shortage	harsh	rigorous	contradiction	lenience

Words That Do Not Match

Identify which of the 5 options A-E matches LEAST WELL in meaning to the word on the left. There is only one best answer. Shade your one chosen answer.

		A	B	C	D	E
10	**action**	operation	movement	measure	calculate	deed
11	**partner**	colleague	teammate	organisation	accomplice	girlfriend

Odd One Out

Each group has four words which can have similar meanings, and one word which is different. Find the odd one out. Shade your one chosen answer.

	A	B	C	D	E
12	grasping	acquisitive	mercenary	avaricious	gripping
13	originator	source	supplier	authority	sauce

Go to the next page 

14

(A)	(B)	(C)	(D)	(E)
ocean	foresee	prophesy	predict	divine

15

(A)	(B)	(C)	(D)	(E)
collude	assist	cooperate	corroborate	join

16

(A)	(B)	(C)	(D)	(E)
offer	arise	occur	happen	befall

17

(A)	(B)	(C)	(D)	(E)
intense	fervent	internal	acute	powerful

Find The Missing Letters

Complete the sentence by identifying the missing letters. Write one letter into each of the large boxes below. After writing each letter, shade its corresponding element in the A-Z block beside it.

18 Maria hastened to make me comfortable while shooing away my tiresome unwanted visitors, and alerting the doctor who was half asleep at his desk in the corner. This nurse was truly a marvel of eff□□□□ncy

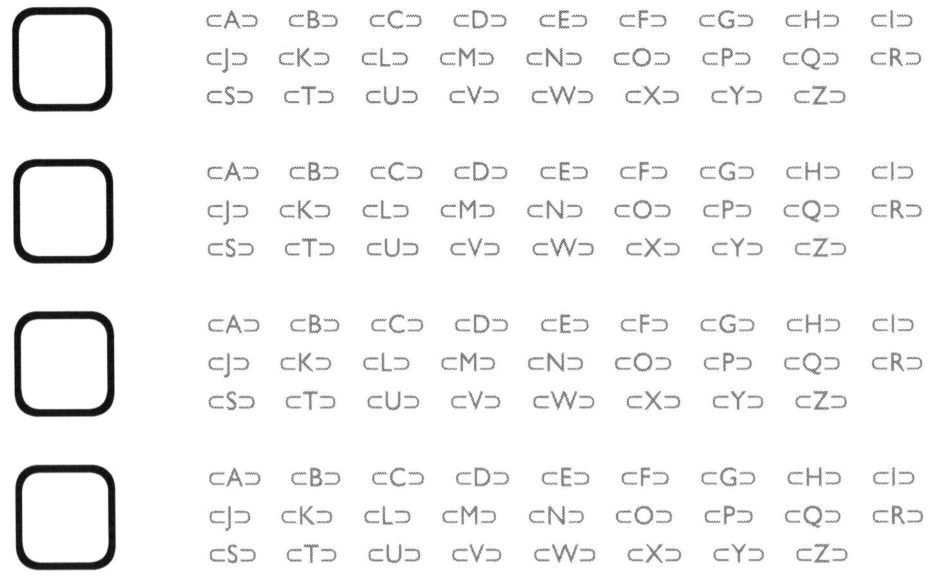

Similar relationships

Each sentence below states that one relationship is similar to another relationship. Choose the word, from options A to E, that completes the sentence best.

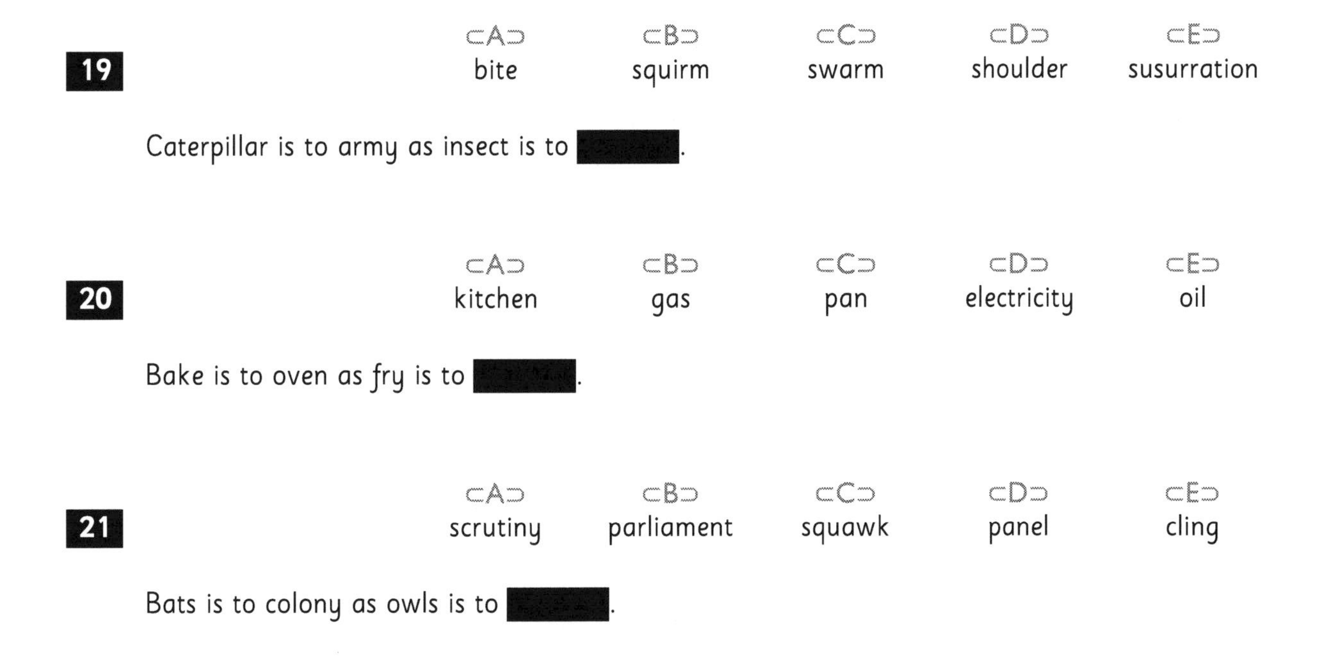

19

A	B	C	D	E
bite	squirm	swarm	shoulder	susurration

Caterpillar is to army as insect is to ______.

20

A	B	C	D	E
kitchen	gas	pan	electricity	oil

Bake is to oven as fry is to ______.

21

A	B	C	D	E
scrutiny	parliament	squawk	panel	cling

Bats is to colony as owls is to ______.

Find The Missing Word

In each of the following pieces of text, one word is missing.
Complete it by choosing the one option A to E which fits best.

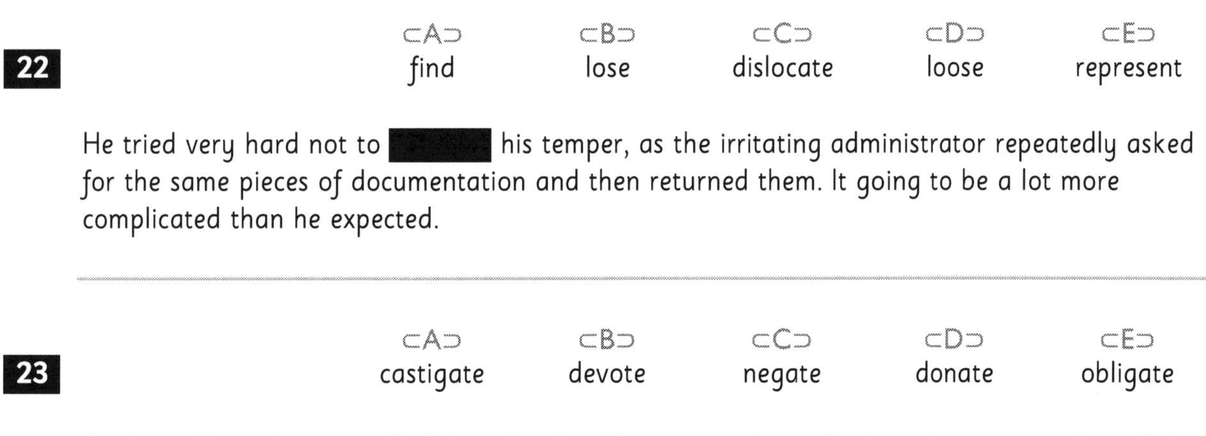

22

A	B	C	D	E
find	lose	dislocate	loose	represent

He tried very hard not to ______ his temper, as the irritating administrator repeatedly asked for the same pieces of documentation and then returned them. It going to be a lot more complicated than he expected.

23

A	B	C	D	E
castigate	devote	negate	donate	obligate

As the tinkling glass signalled that they had for a second time broken the main window of the assembly hall, the headmaster arrived to ______ them for disobeying his very firm instruction after the first occasion.

Go to the next page ➡

24

A	B	C	D	E
selection	lectured	assiduous	assist	slapdash

Caroline had been bottom of the class in Verbal Reasoning last year, but twelve months of ▬▬▬ studying had worked marvels: she now had boosted her score to be in the top five.

25

A	B	C	D	E
balloon	lampoon	interview	disappear	punish

She could not resist the temptation to ▬▬▬ the headmistress, and her imitations were indeed exquisite. Unfortunately standing just around the corner was the victim of this hilarity, and she was not amused.

26

A	B	C	D	E
tiny	horrifying	opulent	misshapen	unfamiliar

Striding into his ▬▬▬ living room, the prince snapped his fingers to summon servants to open the gilded curtains and light the candles in the vast crystal chandeliers.

27

A	B	C	D	E
connote	precise	concise	precede	concede

With three quarters of the votes counted, the young candidate was forced to ▬▬▬ defeat, since his electoral support had evaporated, taking with it his hopes to one day be prime minister.

28

A	B	C	D	E
college	select	collect	section	collage

Putting the twenty cuttings together into a single giant ▬▬▬, she took our outline idea for the new shop and brought it completely to life.

29

A	B	C	D	E
miller	guru	milliner	liner	minimum

Lady Charlotte knew she couldn't be seen again in any of her hat collection as she had already been photographed twice in each one. She could no longer postpone a visit to her ______ to order at least a dozen more.

30

A	B	C	D	E
regular	scintillating	tedious	ugly	handsome

He may not be much to look at, thought Lady Charlotte, but he is a ______ conversationalist, delighting every guest at the party with lively discourse on matters of interest to them. How fortunate that her new hat had arrived just in time for her chance to bump into him again.

This is the end of the training session.

Read the explanations at the back. In the box below, note any words you came across that were unfamiliar, together with a meaning or an example of usage. Practice using these words with adults.

Word	A short sentence *you* have created, using the word

Training Session 34

Matching Words

Identify which word is MOST SIMILAR in meaning to the word on the left. Each question has only one best answer. For each question shade your one chosen answer.

		A	B	C	D	E
1	**staid**	left	remained	solemn	gripped	withheld
2	**forbear**	understand	renounce	grant	descendant	predecessor
3	**conscience**	grounding	calculation	scruples	awake	solidity
4	**structure**	comparison	resignation	divide	form	rhythm
5	**convention**	retention	dispute	nunnery	assembly	innovation
6	**belies**	revise	underpins	abdomens	supports	disproves
7	**project**	obstruct	injection	refusal	needle	undertaking

Opposite Words

Identify which word is MOST OPPOSITE in meaning to the word on the left. Each question has only one best answer. For each question shade your one chosen answer.

		A	B	C	D	E
8	**imperious**	unwanted	haughty	unassuming	unnecessary	bullying
9	**seize**	flowing	grab	lands	clutch	release

Words That Do Not Match

Identify which of the 5 options A-E matches LEAST WELL in meaning to the word on the left. There is only one best answer. Shade your one chosen answer.

		A	B	C	D	E
10	**agreeable**	pleasant	definable	likeable	amiable	gracious
11	**prolific**	teeming	profuse	luxuriant	abundant	suspicious

Odd One Out

Each group has four words which can have similar meanings, and one word which is different. Find the odd one out. Shade your one chosen answer.

	A	B	C	D	E
12	register	dialogue	record	ledger	archive
13	abstruse	arcane	perplexing	esoteric	drizzling

Go to the next page 

	A	B	C	D	E
14	friction	discord	clashing	ripcord	antagonism
15	limited	company	bounded	finite	restricted
16	aid	gamble	abet	foster	advance
17	provocative	inflammatory	rousing	inflammable	agitating

Find The Missing Letters

Complete the sentence by identifying the missing letters. Write one letter into each of the large boxes below. After writing each letter, shade its corresponding element in the A-Z block beside it.

18 Against everything he had said, the flat had no sitting room, cats were not allowed, and the previous tenant had not moved out already. I have never met such a de□□□□ful estate agent in all my long years of sad experience with that profession.

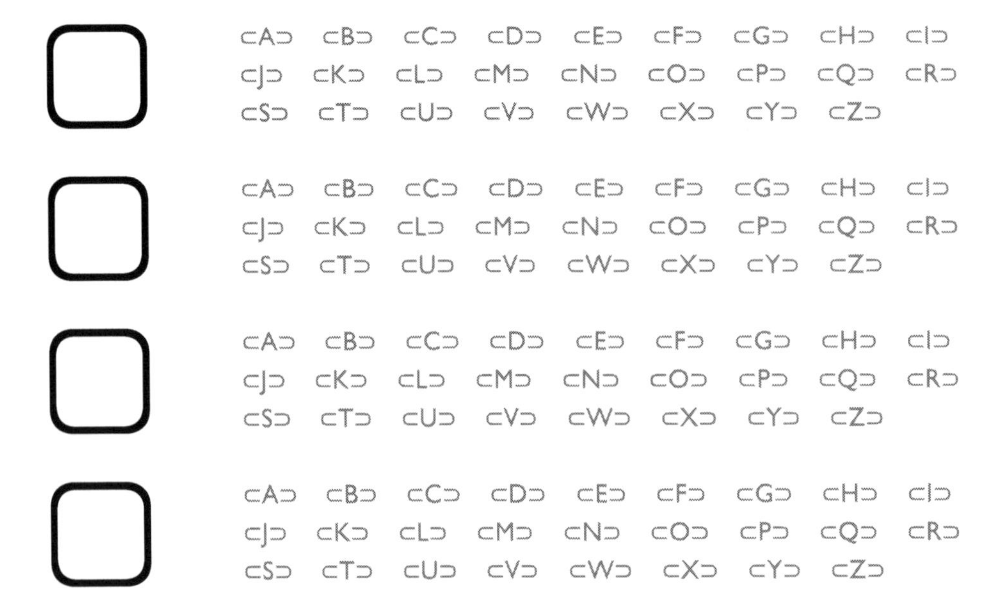

Similar relationships

Each sentence below states that one relationship is similar to another relationship. Choose the word, *from* options A to E, that completes the sentence best.

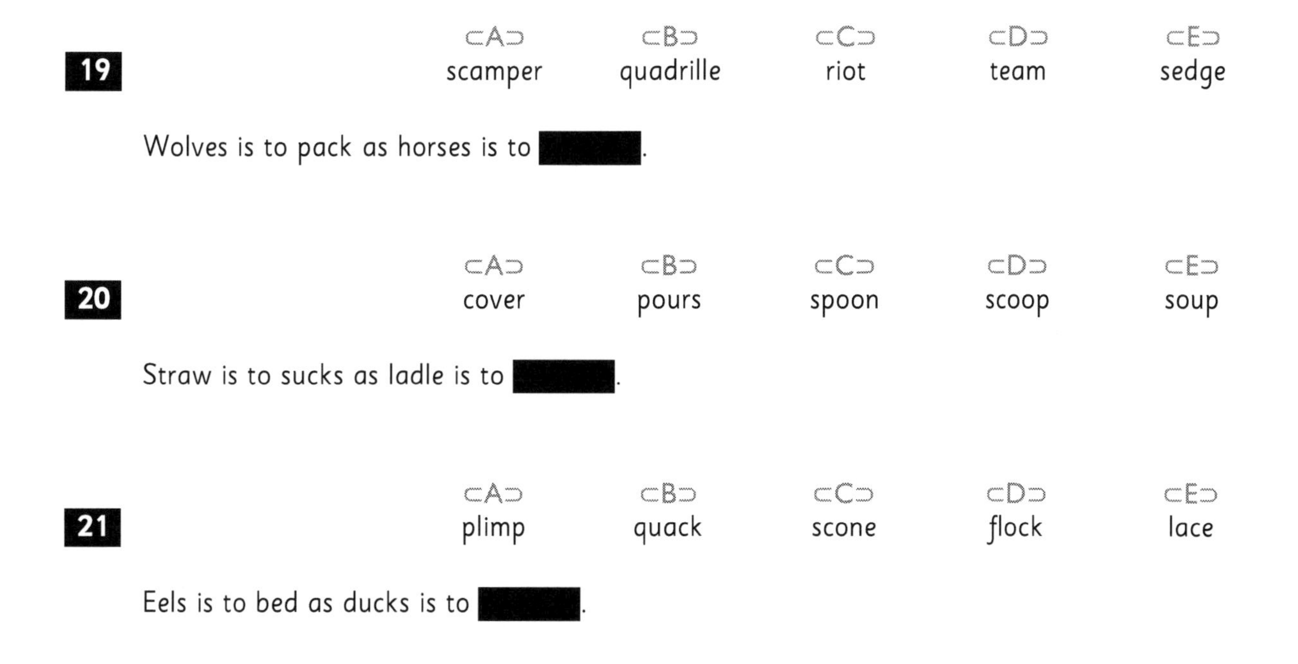

19

A	B	C	D	E
scamper	quadrille	riot	team	sedge

Wolves is to pack as horses is to ______.

20

A	B	C	D	E
cover	pours	spoon	scoop	soup

Straw is to sucks as ladle is to ______.

21

A	B	C	D	E
plimp	quack	scone	flock	lace

Eels is to bed as ducks is to ______.

Find The Missing Word

In each of the following pieces of text, one word is missing.
Complete it by choosing the one option A to E which fits best.

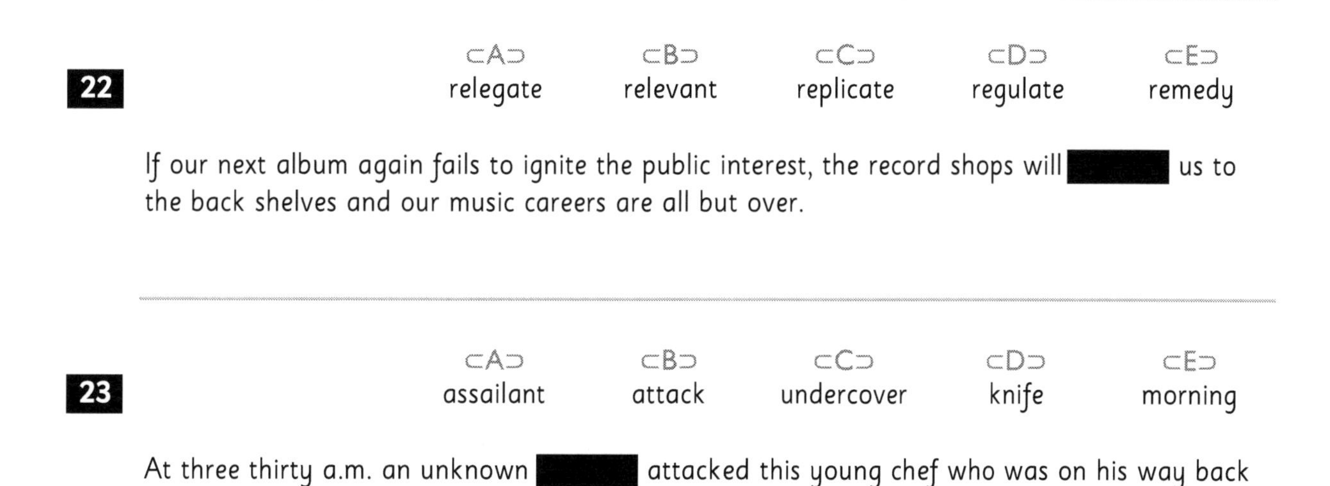

22

A	B	C	D	E
relegate	relevant	replicate	regulate	remedy

If our next album again fails to ignite the public interest, the record shops will ______ us to the back shelves and our music careers are all but over.

23

A	B	C	D	E
assailant	attack	undercover	knife	morning

At three thirty a.m. an unknown ______ attacked this young chef who was on his way back from a night duty shift at the restaurant. While details of the incident are still not clear, we do know that the victim is alive and recovering in hospital.

Go to the next page

24

⊂A⊃	⊂B⊃	⊂C⊃	⊂D⊃	⊂E⊃
goat	rogue	goad	road	load

I just couldn't help it. I took every opportunity to ______ the traffic policeman as I cycled past. After two weeks of this maltreatment, of course he arranged for his friends to be ready to arrest me. The outcome should have been obvious to me.

25

⊂A⊃	⊂B⊃	⊂C⊃	⊂D⊃	⊂E⊃
absent	monotonous	resounding	conspicuous	convenient

Despite the impressive advertising, the lecture was far from inspiring. The content was dull, the delivery ______ and the speaker's engagement with the audience was tepid.

26

⊂A⊃	⊂B⊃	⊂C⊃	⊂D⊃	⊂E⊃
frightened	fringe	odorous	odious	frivolous

Sharon tried to excuse herself from the drama class that she knew would provide an excuse for the ______ bully, Laverne, to mock her hairstyle yet again.

27

⊂A⊃	⊂B⊃	⊂C⊃	⊂D⊃	⊂E⊃
outdoors	uneven	chore	floral	onerous

Agreeing to take on the contract for the new garden was turning out to be a mistake, mused the landscape designer. The unending series of meetings and endless phone calls were becoming very ______, even considering the fine fee being promised.

28

⊂A⊃	⊂B⊃	⊂C⊃	⊂D⊃	⊂E⊃
gargantuan	genuine	garrulous	gardening	gravitas

You have little hope of quiet rest on your upcoming flight to New York. Our new colleague, who will be flying with you, has already built a reputation for being exceptionally ______.

29

⊂A⊃	⊂B⊃	⊂C⊃	⊂D⊃	⊂E⊃
sumptuous	organised	tumultuous	presumptuous	summary

The duke greeted us with extraordinary extravagance. The week of festivities began with a ▇▇▇▇ banquet, bringing together food from all corners of the continent, each dish cooked in a different local style.

30

⊂A⊃	⊂B⊃	⊂C⊃	⊂D⊃	⊂E⊃
terminate	relentless	automate	humanoid	unstoppable

That training workbook was a good read in places and occasionally even mildly amusing, but did stretch my vocabulary annoyingly at every turn. Even as it drew to a close, it could not simply "finish": it had to "▇▇▇▇".

This is the end of the training session.
Read the explanations at the back. In the box below, note any words you came across that were unfamiliar, together with a meaning or an example of usage. Practice using these words with adults.

Word	A short sentence *you* have created, using the word

Explanations for Training Session 18

1 B coincidence

Serendipity means a happy coincidence. The term arises from a Persian tale, The 3 Princes of Serendib, who repeatedly had such events.

2 B pathway

Route means the path by which something travels, occurs or is achieved. This can be an actual physical pathway, or a conceptual series of steps.

3 A tirade

A tirade is a long, angry, and perhaps rambling, speech of complaint; a rant. Synonyms: diatribe, invective, harangue, polemic.

4 B extinguish

Quench means put out a fire or very rapidly cool something, particularly a piece of extremely hot metal.

5 C closeness

Proximity is closeness. This can be either in space or in time or both.

6 C procedure

A protocol is a standard procedure or method for doing something, especially in relation to negotiating or managing something, and most especially for international negotiations or diplomacy.

7 A cheer

Amuse versus bemuse. To amuse is to entertain or to cause to laugh by being funny. To bemuse means to confuse or make bewildered.

8 E permanent

Evanescent means short-lasting, because the item in question passes out of sight, ceases to exist, or people forget it. For example, it may fade away or disappear.

9 D indiscernible

Dazzling means extremely bright. Indiscernible means so subtle or dim that it cannot be detected.

10 D occasion

Schedule (noun) means a plan for an event or series of events. Schedule (verb) means to set dates or times for an event, or formulate the plan for timings within an event.

11 C anger

Content (verb) means make satisfied or content (adjective). Content (noun, emphasis on the first syllable) means the subject or matter of a book, film or similar item.

12 D waterproof

Other than waterproof, all the words mean extremely clean or blameless: they are synonyms of immaculate.

13 D open-minded

Open-minded means willing to consider new thoughts or beliefs. All the other words mean that someone did something in a very superficial, brief or inadequate manner.

14 D night-time

All the other words mean taking a sad or pessimistic view on events.

15 C elusive

Elusive versus illusive. Elusive means difficult to find, understand or capture. Illusive means giving an illusory (false) appearance.

16 C gravelly

Gravelly means containing gravel, or (by analogy) anything very rough and abrasive, including some types of deep voice. The other words are synonyms for gravely (with a single L).

17 B confident

Confident versus confidant. All the other words indicate a friend, with whom secrets (confidences) may be shared. Confident means sure. An intimate is a person on intimate terms.

18 'MMOD': the word is 'accommodate'

Accommodate means to house or contain someone or something. There are two Cs and two Ms. The letter between the M and the D is an O: think of the word "commodious" for a large space.

19 A claw

A cat has paws at the ends of its limbs, and bird has claws.

20 D obscure

Celerity means swiftness. Slow is the adjective for the opposite. Celebrity means fame. Obscure is the adjective for the opposite.

21 C busyness

The true collective noun for ferrets is busyness (with a Y), which has been misspelled frequently as business, besyness, and various alternatives with an F instead of a B.

22 B discursive

Discursive means moving from subject to subject without an apparent plan, rambling and overly long, perhaps including digressions (or side-stories).

23 B wreath

A wreath means a special display of flowers, often in a horse-shoe or ring shape. Rarely, it means a curl of smoke or mist. In contrast, wreathe is a verb and means to surround or encircle something.

24 C except

Except means exclude, do not count, or leave out. Accept is to receive or agree to something. Deviate could only be correct if the word "you" after the blank wasn't there.

25 A discordant

Discordant means disagreeing, contradicting or (especially of music) clashing.

26 A queue

A queue is a line of people waiting in order of their arrival, for goods or service.

27 D practice

In British English, the verb is practise and the noun is practice. The two different words sound identical. The pattern is the same for advise (verb)/advice (noun) and license (verb)/licence (noun).

28 E turgid

Turgid, in biology, refers to a plant stem full of fluid and therefore rigid. The word also describes text that is too wordy, complex or difficult. Turbid means cloudiness of a liquid caused by particles.

29 B desert

Desert means a waterless land. Desert (verb) means to abandon a person. It can be used figuratively for a skill that becomes suddenly unavailable. Dessert is a light dish served after the main meal.

30 C erode

To erode is to rub away, either forming a channel or gap, or removing something that was there before. Wear is the correct concept but would need an additional word such as "out" or "down".

Explanations for Training Session 19

1 C growth

Proliferation means an increase in the amount of something. It can refer to living creatures (such as weeds) or habits of people.

2 D crucial

Pivotal means of major importance to the success of a greater aim. For example, attending the examination on time is pivotal to the greater aim of scoring well.

3 E rife

Pervasive means widely spread throughout something. It is used most often in relation to something undesirable. Rife has a similar meaning.

4 D warning

To superstitious people, an omen is a warning from a supernatural source of something that will happen in future. More widely the word is used to indicate any indicator of the future.

5 A narrate

To recite is to speak aloud a story or poem. The word carries the suggestion that this is done entirely from memory, rather than by reading from notes.

6 E productive

Fertile, in relation to land, means capable of generating large amounts of plant life or crops for human consumption. In relation to people, it means capable of having children.

7 C artificial

Contrived means either specially made (e.g. a tool contrived to achieve a task) or not natural, genuine or spontaneous (for example a contrived excuse).

8 C permanent

Fleeting means for only a very short time. It can describe a thought that passes through one's head only briefly (a fleeting thought) or a brief opportunity to see something (a fleeting glimpse).

9 A depression

Euphoria is a state of being extremely happy or very excited. It can occur naturally or be induced by drugs.

10 B strength

Virtue is a pattern of behaviour of high moral standards, including honesty, thoughtfulness, selflessness and purity. Strength is also desirable but need not be associated with virtue.

11 A answer

A counterfeit (noun) is a copy of an original item, produced with the intention of deceiving people into mistaking it for the original. To counterfeit (verb) is to make a counterfeit item.

12 E specious

Specious means at first sounding reasonable, but on further examination, untrue. The word spacious, not an option in this question, matches the other words.

13 B pulsatile

Plausible (of an idea) means sounding reasonable or believable. The same word used of a person means something more: sounding reasonable but being deceptive or misleading. Pulsatile means pulsing or throbbing.

14 B discover

All the words mean to release some information that had been kept secret, except discover which means to obtain.

15 B shrink

All the other words mean a formal agreement. Contract has another meaning, namely to become smaller which matches shrink. However in this question shrink is the odd one out.

16 B perspex

All the words mean confuse or mystify, except perspex which is a form of transparent plastic.

17 A stick

All the words mean that different things are in agreement, except stick.

18 'DIEN': the word is 'audience'

An audience was originally a group of people listening to a musical or vocal performance (from the Latin audire to hear), now extended to cover people watching too.

19 B woods

Gilded means relating to gold. Sylvan means relating to woodland (not silver).

20 E hog

A hart is a male deer. A hog is a male pig.

21 B suspicion

Effrontery is behaviour that causes offence. Furtiveness (behaving like a thief) is behaviour that leads to suspicion.

22 D hers

Indicating ownership using possessive pronouns does not require an apostrophe. It is no more needed for hers than for mine or his.

23 C coerce

Coerce means force or threaten someone so that they do something.

24 D inflict

Inflict means deliver a damaging injury or wound on someone, for example by a kick or punch or using a sword or similar weapon.

25 A cue

A cue is a signal that it is time for something to happen, especially during a play or the recording of a film. Alternatively it is a stick used in sports such as snooker or billiards to knock a ball.

26 E despicable

Despicable is an adjective used for people who should be despised or condemned, because of their actions. It can also apply to actions of that nature.

27 A expect

Expect is to think in advance that somethinq will happen. Accept is to receive or agree to something.

28 A bonnet

The bonnet is lid to the front compartment of a car, which in most cases is where the engine is. None of the other options describes a plausible, precise description of a place to investigate such a sound.

29 A disperse

Disperse means spread out over a wide region. It can refer to individuals or, in chemistry, a substance being spread out in a liquid.

30 A censure

To censure is to formally state that someone has behaved incorrectly, and (in some cases) to impose a punishment.

Explanations for Training Session 20

1 D predict

Prophesy versus prophecy. Prophesy is the verb (relatively rare); prophecy is the noun (relatively common). Respectively they indicate the process of prediction, and the prediction itself.

2 C strong

Potent means powerful or strong, exerting a large effect. A portent (with an R) is a sign of the future, or an omen.

3 D plot

Circumstances can conspire (work together in a harmful way) such as extreme cold and high winds. People can conspire (work together, especially in secret) to do something criminal or evil.

4 A profusion

Abundance means a great quantity of something, especially if this is more than is needed. The corresponding verb is abound: "Sweets abounded in Soraya's house; little wonder that she was so rotund."

5 D plentiful

Ample means plenty or more than enough. It can also be used more specifically to indicate large size (especially of a container), for example an ample room or bed, or that someone is overweight.

6 C allot

Portion (noun) means a piece or share, but as a verb it means the process of sharing out or dividing something. This question doesn't give an option using it as a noun.

7 E uncertain

Obscure (adjective) can mean (about a fact) that it is unknown or uncertain, and (about a statement) that it is difficult to understand, perhaps because it is badly worded. Obscure (verb) means conceal.

8 B eternal

Ephemeral means short-lasting, for example in relation to a habit that is popular only for a short time, or a plant species whose life span is short.

9 E disbelief

Credence is acceptance of something as true, by a particular group of people. It is distinct from whether the speaker believes something might be true, which is termed credibility.

10 B inventive

Ingenuous versus ingenious. IngenUous means innocent, simple, uncontrived. Ingenlous means (of an idea) very clever or (of a person) bright, gifted, able, resourceful and skilful.

11 D incorporate

Scrutinise means examine very carefully and thoroughly; peruse, study, survey, inspect, probe, analyse, dissect, review, audit.

12 E aloof

All the words indicate great height, except aloof which means keeping oneself away from others.

13 C learning

All the other words mean a tendency or liking for a thing or a point of view/

14 B accuracy

All the other words mean a person with a habit if cheating, stealing or committing some other crime.

15 A thimble

All the other words indicate liveliness and fast, delicate movement.

16 E demand

All the other words indicate the power to exert control. To demand only indicates that one can ask for something (perhaps roughly), but it does not mean that that thing will be given.

17 E indefinite

All the other words are verbs for continuing a state of affairs into the future.

18 'HYTH': the word is 'rhythm'

The word rhythm, meaning the strong repeating element of a musical piece, is one of the most frequently misspelled words in English. If it helps, break it down in to a rhythm of 2 sets of 3 letters: rHy, tHm.

19 B worthwhile

Deferential is the opposite of rude. The opposite of futile (something that cannot succeed) is worthwhile (which is something that may succeed and be useful).

20 A exciting

An idyll is a description of a scene that is peaceful. A drama is a description of a scene that is exciting.

21 C cart

A rocket can hurtle. The vehicle that trundles, amongst the collection given, is a cart.

22 D enterprise

An enterprise is a business, a major project that is embarked upon or the characteristic of a person which makes them willing to set up such a business or project. Spelling tip: Remember the first R.

23 D allowed

Allowed means permitted. Aloud means out loud, such as reading some words by speaking them rather than silently.

24 E curtail

Curtail means bring to an end or shorten. It can mean halt an ongoing process before it has finished normally, or cause people to hurry up and finish early, or cut off a part of an object.

25 C blossom

In relation to plants, to blossom means to develop flowers. Figuratively, it means to develop or advance in skill, beauty or other attributes.

26 E eponym

An eponym is a name given to a thing or creature, to recognise the discoverer or inventor. For example, Halley's Comet is named after Edmund Halley, the astronomer.

27 B clamour

A clamour is the noise of many people shouting, or any combination of many noises which are not individually discernible.

28 D women's

It was the lunch that belonged to the women, so write women, and add an apostrophe and an s.

29 C daunt

To daunt is to frighten.

30 A amicable

Amicable describes a relationship between two or more people. This word should not be used for one person in isolation. The similar word indicating that a person is generally friendly is "amiable".

Explanations for Training Session 21

1 D restrained

Temperate (of a climate) means lacking extremes of heat or cold or (of a person) means having a moderate, level-headed personality rather than being excitable or hot-headed.

2 D discerning

Judicious is related to the word "judge" and means showing good judgement. Judicious is commonly used to describe wise use of limited resources, or intervention whose perfect timing maximises its effect.

3 D pitiful

If a person is pathetic, it means other people pity them, especially if the reason is that they are weak, vulnerable or in a desperate situation.

4 B occupy

Inhabit means to occupy a space or live in a place.

5 A passing

Temporary means not permanent but lasting only for a particular period of time. The word, especially when abbreviated to "temp", is also used specifically for temporary workers.

6 A retain

To withhold is to refuse permission for someone to have something that they have requested or would normally receive, such as a payment.

7 B contemplative

Pensive (of a person) indicates that they appear to be thinking deeply about something, making them speak less than usual or be distracted.

8 A easy

An enigma is a difficult puzzle; enigmatic describes a puzzling person or thing.

9 A retard

To expedite is to speed up a process or make it happen earlier than would otherwise be the case.

10 B agree

To refuse is to indicate that unwillingness to do something, receive something ("I have to refuse your kind offer") or give something ("She refused him water.") It also means rubbish, garbage and trash.

11 B cross

In some sports, the person who oversees the game, ensuring fare play, is the umpire. The umpire (noun) ensures fair play according to the rules. The process is called umpiring.

12 A insolvent

All the other words mean lazy. Insolvent means bankrupt, i.e. having debts that are too great to pay.

13 D abdicate

All the other words mean continue to be alive. Abdicate means to give up a role, especially that of king or queen.

14 E prisoner

All the other words mean a thought about what might be the case, but without factual confirmation.

15 D moose

All the other words mean being sad or miserable, especially in interactions with others.

16 C capability

All the other words are adverbs for the quality with which something was done. Capability means the capacity (or ability) to do something.

17 C minimalist

All the other words mean mild-mannered, unassuming or undemanding. Minimalist indicates that the person is not withholding demands but themselves do not want anything.

18 'ERI': the word is 'eerie'

Eerie means strange, mysterious and frightening. Its spelling is, coincidentally, unsettling too, and is best learned by heart, as it is one of the most frequently misspelled words in the English language.

19 E action

After incarceration (imprisonment) comes release. After hesitation comes action.

20 D gaggle

Gaggle is the collective noun for a group of geese on the ground. When in flight, they are called a team, a wedge or a skein.

21 E ambush

Strange but true: the collective noun for tigers is ambush. Options for gnats are cloud, horde and swarm.

22 A sporadic

Sporadic means infrequent and irregular. It is a better contrast to daily than spartan, which indicates letters that are short or lacking in detail (rather than infrequent).

23 D dismantle

Dismantle means separate into pieces, in relation to something complex which is made of parts.

24 E storey

Storey means a level or floor in a building with many floors. A story is a tale. They are unrelated. Here, colour on a staircase or elevator would not help identify the level in the building.

25 A capitol

In some countries, a capitol is a particular building which houses the top level of the government. In all countries, the capital is the formally designated main or leading city.

26 D bittersweet

Bittersweet means mixing happiness with sadness, especially in relation to a story. It can also refer to a drink or food that is initially sweet, but some time later leaves a bitter aftertaste

27 B grizzly

Grizzly is a type of brown bear found in North America. Grisly means horrible, ghastly or revolting, in relation to a crime or a scene and especially of a murder.

28 E epiphany

An epiphany is a sudden realisation that transforms one's ability to solve a problem.

29 A spurn

To spurn is to reject emphatically and give the impression that the offer is unwanted, unneeded or beneath one's dignity to accept.

30 A humane

Humane means showing kindness or compassion, often in relation to animals, but also to prisoners or other vulnerable individuals. Synonyms include benevolent, kind-hearted, gentle, considerate, humanitarian.

Explanations for Training Session 22

1 B dangle

To suspend is to hang or dangle something. It can also mean temporarily prohibit someone from doing their job or going to school, or temporarily cancel a rule, or temporarily delay a process.

2 D lethargic

Sluggish means moving slowly or lacking interest in activity. It can also indicate a state of tiredness, lethargy, lifelessness, or lack of interest (apathy).

3 B weight

A thing with significance has importance, value, weight, import or seriousness. When referring to an event or a statement, significance refers to what that event or statement means.

4 C impertinent

Insolent means rude and lacking respect. Synonyms are impertinent, impudent, cheeky, rude, impolite and insubordinate.

5 A forbidden

Illicit versus elicit. Illicit means banned by rules (which may be the law of a country or the customary standards of behaviour in a group). Elicit means cause something to happen.

6 E pamper

To indulge is to give in easily to a temptation, or to a request, or to allow another person to have a pleasurable experience that they request.

7 C divine

Sacred means relating to God or gods, or related to religious matters. The word may relate to religious activities or objects or pieces of land that have special religious significance.

8 D unselective

Discerning means able to distinguish subtleties; being thoughtful and having good judgement.

9 A hesitant

Gung-ho, derived from a Chinese term "gōng hé", meaning "work together", was adopted by the US Marines as a battle cry in the 1940s, and now generally means very enthusiastic and perhaps excessively so.

10 C register

To approve is to officially give agreement for something, such as a request, a payment or permission to do something. To approve of someone is to consider them satisfactory or good; to praise or esteem them.

11 C envious

Anxious means having worry, nervousness or unease about something in the future; worried, concerned, overwrought, tense, distressed, fretful, agitated, troubled, perturbed, apprehensive.

12 B subtracting

All the other words mean making few demands or not claiming high status.

13 A unkempt

All the other words mean incompetent. Unkempt means untidy or not looked after well.

14 C ceremony

All the other words mean to walk or behave in a boastful or conceited way. A ceremony may have such characteristics but in general does not have to.

15 C substance

All the other words indicate a plan or programme which contains steps that are to be carried out.

16 A morale

Moral versus morale. Moral (adjective) means regarding the distinction between good and bad behaviour. Moral (noun) is the lesson from a story or experience. Morale is confidence or enthusiasm within a group.

17 E exploit

All the words mean take care of a resource, saving some for later, except for exploit.

18 'IERC': the word is 'fierce'

Fierce means being or appearing to be violent or aggressive.

19 D plants

Milk provides nutrition for a baby. Manure provides nutrition for plants: not the whole farm and certainly not directly for the farmer.

20 E pack

The collective noun for flamingoes, because of their curious one-legged standing pose, is the stand. For coyote (a dog-like animal) it is pack.

21 A limb

A car is one type of vehicle. Similarly, an arm is one of the two types of limb: arm and leg.

22 A brawn

Brawn means muscular strength, as opposed to intelligence in how this strength is used to achieve an aim.

23 D dissipate

Dissipate means to gradually disappear. For money, it implies careless or wasteful usage. In this question, note that snow melts, running away as water rather than evaporating directly to gas.

24 E discontent

Discontent is a sense of not being satisfied or happy, generally in relation to something such as a service, environment or product. The movements being described are characteristic of discontented people.

25 B differential

Differential means different between different elements. For example, a pay differential means that people are paid different amounts. Deferential means behaving in a very polite way.

26 D censor

To censor is to limit what can be published, on grounds of the public benefit, or to preserve secrecy.

27 B degrade

To degrade is to deteriorate in quality.

28 E counsel

A council is a group of people, whereas to counsel (with an S and an E) is to give advice.

29 D bland

Bland means lacking in features or flavour. Regarding a person, it indicates lack of depth or meaning to a relationship or interaction.

30 D patronising

Patronising is superficial kindness but in a way that makes the recipient feel inferior. Awful would fit the sense of the sentence, but starts with a vowel, which conflicts with the preceding word.

Explanations for Training Session 23

1 A elevation

Altitude means height above the ground (or sea level). This is different from attitude which means the habitual way a person thinks about something or interacts with someone.

2 A congregate

Assemble means put together components to make something, or (of several people) come together into one place for a purpose.

3 B outdo

To surpass is to be better than something or greater than something. A special usage is "to surpass oneself" which means to be better than ever before.

4 B prediction

Prophesy versus prophecy. Prophesy is the verb (relatively rare); prophecy is the noun (relatively common). Respectively they indicate the process of prediction, and the prediction itself.

5 C statement

Testimony is an official statement, which may be delivered orally or in writing, especially in a court of law. The word is also used figuratively to refer to evidence of a fact.

6 D decency

Propriety is the act of behaving according to generally accepted standards of what is proper, in terms of decency, modesty or fairness.

7 E basic

Rudimentary means basic or elementary. It can apply to the level of a subject being studied, or the level of development of an item or facilities.

8 C defame

To defame is to make untrue adverse statements about a person harms their public status. Although the other options may be linked to defamation, they are not a direct opposite to the verb (or noun) praise.

9 D underwhelm

To disappoint is to fail to fulfil the expectations that had been in place beforehand.

10 E apprehensive

Mete means give justice, especially if it is punishment. Apportion means give, with emphasis on distributing appropriately amongst several people or organisations.

11 B serve

To appease means to make someone less angry by giving in to their demands (conciliate, pacify, propitiate, palliate, reconcile, allay, placate). Separately it can mean to fulfil or satisfy a demand or need.

12 B irascible

All the other words mean not showing extreme emotions.

13 C insistence

All the other words mean a reason to do something.

14 E bear

Bear versus bare. Bear means withstand, or a type of large mammal. Bare is the word that matches the others.

15 D reluctant

Reluctant versus reticent. Reluctant means unwilling to do something. Reticent means quiet and uncommunicative. A reticent person may be reluctant to speak, but the words are different.

16 A cheap

All the other words mean unvarying and protected.

17 B conserve

All the other words mean use up. Conserve means keep aside for the future.

18 'AURA': the word is 'restaurant'

If you are having difficulty spelling restaurant, it might help to know it comes from a French word restaurer, meaning to restore.

19 A fill

Attack and retreat are opposite processes, as are dig and fill.

20 D pod

Pod is the collective noun for dolphins. Alternatives are school and team.

21 E ear

The ear has a part named the lobe, and a finger has a part named the nail.

22 E coarse

Coarse language is rude or uncultured. It is possible that someone may want to avoid young children hearing foreign languages; however it is far more plausible that the request was to avoid coarse language.

23 E children's

The concentration belonged to the children, so it is the children's concentration. It cannot be a single child alone, because the latter part of the sentence refers to "their".

24 C berth

A berth is a bunk or accommodation on a ship. Birth means the process of being born.

25 B disseminate

Disseminate means distribute widely, and is most commonly used in relation to information.

26 A extended

Longer fits the meaning but would be preceded by "a" not "an". The other words fit grammatically but do not fit the meaning as well as "extended" which is in good contrast to "short".

27 B unconscious

Unconscious means without actively thinking about it. The word also is used to describe people deeply sedated and unaware of their surroundings, for example after an accident or during a surgical procedure.

28 E cord

A cord is a piece of string or a biological part that resembles a piece of string. A chord is a group of musical notes that are played together to produce a pleasant sound.

29 B complaisant

Complaisant means willing to accept in order to please others or go along with requests. It is distinct from complacent which means smug or excessively satisfied with one's achievement or status.

30 E a long

A long versus along. "A long" means an object with a great extent in one horizontal direction. Along is a preposition indicating movement in a continuous trajectory, or an approximately horizontal arrangement.

Explanations for Training Session 24

1 C peculiarity

Idiosyncrasy means a particular manner of behaviour or habit of thought that is special to that individual.

2 D rejoice

Exult versus exalt. To exUlt is to rejoice, for example when one hears good news. To exAlt is to glorify, for example in a religious ceremony.

3 E dull

Mundane means uninteresting, unexciting or dull. Synonyms include tedious, monotonous, tiresome, routine, ordinary, customary.

4 C sombre

Subdued (of a person) means saddened or quieter than usual, (of a rebellion) halted or abolished, or (of lighting) mild rather than bright.

5 E ascertain

Determine means either decide something will happen in a particular way ("I determined that the class would formally start at 6 pm") or find something out by a process of study and calculation.

6 E common

Prevalent means present, or used, widely. Synonyms are pervasive, ubiquitous, prevailing, frequent, widespread or ordinary

7 D brave

Valiant means courageous, bold, determined or heroic.

8 A convict

Exonerate means to declare someone to be blameless for something that has gone wrong or a crime that has been committed.

9 D alleviate

To exacerbate is to make a situation or problem worse than before

10 C terminate

Overt means obvious, outward, plain, visible and public. Manifest (adjective) has a similar meaning.

11 A similar

A parable is a simple tale designed to make clear a more complex lesson on right versus wrong, or good versus evil.

12 D operative

All the other words mean that there is something wrong with the item being described.

13 C charm

All the other words indicate severe dislike or ill will.

14 C diagonal

All the other words indicate that something has not been confirmed but is merely being guessed at or imagined.

15 B pacific

All the other words indicate one precise individual that is different from others. Pacific means peaceful (and is a common mispronunciation of specific).

16 E aggressive

All the other words mean simple, plain and devoid of luxury.

17 E transparent

All the other words mean very small, limited or inadequate. Transparent refers to transmission of light being good.

18 'GIEN': the word is 'hygiene'

Hygiene means standards of cleanliness that help prevent infectious disease and thereby preserve health.

19 B caravan

Caravan is the collective noun for camels.

20 A trousers

Commonly, shirts are fastened with buttons and, of the options, it is trousers that are most frequently fastened with a zip (albeit almost always with other methods simultaneously).

21 C bouquet

The collective noun for pelicans is a pod. For pheasants it is bouquet (main term), but also head, nest, nide or nye.

22 E crestfallen

Crestfallen means disappointed or sad after an expectation was not met. Synonyms are forlorn, glum, gloomy, downcast, despondent, disconsolate, broken-hearted, miserable, unhappy, woebegone.

23 E clemency

Clemency means leniency or mercy: giving a lighter punishment.

24 D deferential

Deferential means very polite and respectful. Differential means different between different elements. For example, a pay differential means that different people are paid different amounts.

25 B unthinkable

Unthinkable means completely unacceptable and wrong, even at the most basic and simple level.

26 D blasphemy

Blasphemy means speech against god or things that are considered sacred or holy. Figuratively this is applied to speech against what a group considers certainly true and necessary for its own existence.

27 B camaraderie

Only dispute, camaraderie and enjoyment are nouns. Dispute does not fit the meaning well. Passengers more likely felt camaraderie (togetherness in a shared situation) than enjoyment when they were delayed.

28 B levy

To levy is to impose a tax, a fine, or a charge on a person or organisation.

29 D cavorting

Cavort means dance, or jump around in an excited manner. The term is mainly used to indicate displeasure at the activity.

30 B canvass

Canvass means ask people for support for one option in an election or vote. A canvas is the surface on which a painting is painted, or the material of which such a surface is made.

Explanations for Training Session 25

1 B bend

Stoop means to bend forwards and downwards (for example, to pick something up from the floor). It also means to do something of a low standard: "In the end, he had to stoop to cheating."

2 A affect

Influence (noun) means the ability to affect something or someone, or it means that effect itself. As a verb it means the process of having that effect.

3 E aware

Conscious versus conscience. Conscious means knowing, being awake, or being aware. Conscience (or scruples) is the human judgement that distinguishes right from wrong.

4 A advantage

Benefit means the profit obtained, or advantage achieved, by doing something. It can also mean a payment from a government to a person in need. As a verb it means to gain an advantage.

5 C partner

To associate with someone means to be together with them in work or leisure, or to put two things together in one's mind. As a noun it means someone who is associated with someone else.

6 E lowly

Inferior (adjective) means lower in status, either because of lower quality, or of a lower standing in a hierarchical organisation. As a noun it means a person or thing that is inferior.

7 B small

Minor (adjective) means of less significance or importance. As a noun it means a person that has not yet become an adult.

8 B individualistic

Gregarious means preferring to be in groups rather than be alone.

9 E clashing

Euphonious means having a pleasing sound, which could mean a single note or voice, or a combination of many, and either a single instant in time, or a prolonged duration such as a piece of music.

10 E panicked

Sanguine means remaining positive in an adverse situation. Other synonyms than those listed include upbeat, bullish, cheerful, cheery, bright.

11 B deduct

To resolve is to find a solution to a problem or dispute. Separately it can mean (verb) make a firm decision to do a certain thing, or (noun) that decision itself.

12 D snap

All the other words mean a gap in long process such as a play or a game.

13 B mountain

All the other words mean the amount of territory ruled or governed by a leader or a government.

14 B despicable

All the other words mean responsible, reliable and trustworthy.

15 E solace

All the other words indicate the state of being alone. Solace means relief, comfort or consolation when very distressed or sad.

16 E rejoicing

All the other words indicate reducing bad feelings of another person; rejoicing means having a positive feeling oneself.

17 D pleasant

All the other words indicate quantity or level of quality to be enough. Pleasant describes an emotional reaction which is different from a description of a quantity.

18 'EIGN': the word is 'foreign'

Foreign means from or to another country. The spelling is unusual because it was changed in the 16th century from a simpler spelling (foren or forein) to match the spelling of sovereign.

19 A convocation

The collective noun for eagles is convocation.

20 C soup

Take care with the direction of the relationship. Furry is a possible description of a cat (noun). Look for a noun that can be described as liquid (adjective). Only soup fits.

21 E knot

The collective noun for squirrels is dray, scurry or colony. For toads it is knot.

22 D balmy

Balmy refers to weather that is pleasantly warm. Barmy is an informal term indicating crazy or mad.

23 B currency

Lacking knowledge or awareness would indeed be a disadvantage, but the best contrast with the wallet stuffed with pounds would be a lack of local currency (money that was valid in that place).

24 A calamity

Calamity means disaster. Only that option fits the sentence grammatically, although other options may have the correct general meaning.

25 B cite

Cite means refer precisely to detailed evidence.

26 E wreathe

Wreathe (verb) means surround or encircle with decorations (e.g. flowers) or toxic substances such as fumes. Wreath (noun) means a special flower display for a grave or monument, or a curl of smoke or mist.

27 D epic

An epic was originally a long poem relayed orally. Later it meant any very long poem. Then it applied to any very long or complex film. Now it is coming into use for any very large task or excellent thing.

28 A disparity

A disparity is a large or unreasonable difference between two things.

29 D deity

A deity is a god or a being having the characteristics of a god.

30 E canvas

Canvas is the material used by artists to paint on, to make paintings. A canvas is the term for a piece of canvas ready for such use. To canvass is to seek support in an election.

Explanations for Training Session 26

1 D painstaking

Meticulous means precise, very careful and highly attentive to small details. It refers to a person or the detailed work that they do.

2 B perfumed

Fragrant means having a smell that is pleasing; scented, perfumed, aromatic, nice-smelling.

3 E scorn

Contempt means scorn, disrespect or disdain: the feeling that someone or something is of such a low quality or has such bad behaviour that they should not even be considered.

4 B insulting

Impudent versus imprudent. Impudent means rude, insulting, or lacking respect for another person. It is typically used of a person or of an action or remark. Imprudent means careless or unwise.

5 E penetrating

Incisive (when applied to a person, thought or remark) means intelligent and (figuratively) cutting directly to the important issue in a manner that makes it clear to others.

6 D legitimate

Legal means allowed by law or relating to the law or procedures of law.

7 A safeguard

Ensure means to make certain that something will happen or will exist. This is different from insure which means to provide compensation when a thing happens (or fails to happen).

8 D original

A hackneyed phrase is one that has been overused and is unoriginal.

9 C private

Public means relating to a large community, open to everyone, run by the government or at shared expense.

10 D silent

Voluminous means very large. Of writing, it indicates there are many words and hints they may be in excess of requirements. Of clothing, it indicates it is very loose. It does not mean loud.

11 B thorn

To ramble is to walk at leisure in a countryside environment. A ramble is such a walk. To ramble can separately mean to speak or write in a lengthy and disorganised manner.

12 E cabin

All the other words can be verbs for to stay at a place. Cabin is (only) a noun.

13 C inflammatory

Inflammable (and flammable) versus inflammatory. Confusingly inflammABLE and flammABLE mean the same, which is easily set on fire. InflammATORY means causing (or intended to cause) angry feelings.

14 E business

All the other words indicate the coming together of several people for a purpose.

15 A subterranean

All the other words mean deception, trickery, misleading, dishonesty, cheating, ruse, sham, ploy and artifice.

16 B restorer

All the other words indicate someone who follows after an earlier person.

17 C insipid

All the other words mean slow-moving, lazy or feeling tired or unenergetic. Insipid means weak in the sense of being dilute or thin.

18 'HEIS': the word is 'atheism'

Atheism is the belief that there is no god, and is a contrast to theism which is the belief that there is a god or there are gods. It is derived from the Greek a- (without) and theos (god).

19 C cool

Sonorous means having a pleasant deep sound. To whistle is to make a high pitched sound. Similarly warm and cool are opposites.

20 C cellphone

Take care with the direction of the relationship. The nib is part of a pen, and is essential for its working. Likewise, the battery is part of a cellphone (and no other option), and is essential for its working.

21 D shoal

The best collective nouns for fish are shoal and school.

22 B complacent

Complacent means excessively satisfied with one's own position and achievements, and lacking critical attention.

23 D serial

If the headmaster was not intending to be funny, he intended his sentence to refer to a series of offences, i.e. a serial offender, and not someone who causes offence using breakfast cereal.

24 B Let's

Here, let's is an abbreviation for "let us". This is completely different from the word lets, which means permits, for example, "the law lets people drive from the age of 16."

25 A adieu

Adieu is a term for goodbye or farewell, originally French.

26 C charismatic

Charismatic means having powerful charm which can compel others to your way of thinking, and perhaps to obey you.

27 D story

A story is a description of events for entertainment or education, or an article in a newspaper or magazine. A storey is a level in a building. Casement means window.

28 B brevity

Brevity is the noun for brief. The story was long and the speaker was suggesting to make it or other stories shorter in future.

29 B all together

The teachers wanted to keep the children together. Which children? All of them. Therefore it is two separate words: all together. Altogether is a different word, meaning totally or completely, or in total.

30 A site

A site is a place. Sight is the process of seeing or the ability to see. To cite is to refer to a piece of evidence.

Explanations for Training Session 27

1 C country

Rural means relating to the countryside. It can refer to people, the land, or activities (especially farming). The word is used to distinguish those from the corresponding elements in built-up areas.

2 B contemplation

Consideration means detailed thought about something. It is implied that this might take some time. In law, consideration means a payment in return for something else.

3 B basis

A principle is a basis or fundamental fact, upon which a complex arrangement of policies or beliefs can be built. A princiPAL is a head teacher or other leader.

4 B rule

Reign means to be king or queen. It also refers to the period of time during which a king or queen holds that status.

5 A strategy

Policy is the standard strategy applied for handling a situation, by an organisation, government, company or individual. For example: "My policy is not to answer calls from withheld numbers."

6 E overthrow

Revolution means a complete overturning of an established system, often by force. Most commonly it refers to a dramatic change of government system. It can also refer to the process of turning in a circle.

7 E range

Scope means the range of a subject, or the freedom to act on a subject. With a literal meaning of to view, it is also means to examine carefully (by sight).

8 E ordinary

Quaint means having old-fashioned charm, or strange and unusual, especially if the peculiar properties make the thing amusing.

9 E sound

Insane means having serious mental illness that causes abnormal perception or behaviour. Figuratively it means an idea is obviouslyS unsuitable. One meaning of sound is correct, suitable and solid.

10 D refuse

A sanctuary is a place of safety that gives protection from punishment, persecution or pursuit. It also has a specific meaning of nature reserve.

11 D sucking

Soothing means having the effect of inducing calm, reducing pain or easing discomfort. Mollifying has similar meanings.

12 B triplicate

All the other words mean minor or lacking in importance.

13 A poultry

All the other words mean of little or no importance; minor. Poultry means birds reared for eating or egg laying.

14 B message

All the other words indicate something that is brief and to the point. They may relate to a message, but the word message itself does not carry that meaning.

15 E abdicate

All the other words mean reduce tension or tightness, for example of a belt or rope. Abdicate means give up the position of being king or queen.

16 C everyday

All the other words indicate rarity. Everyday means commonplace or often seen.

17 B electrical

All the other words mean happening at the same time.

18 'LIEN': the word is 'client'

A client is a person using the services of a professional such as a lawyer.

19 C brood

The collective noun for finches is charm or chirm; for chicks it is brood or clutch.

20 E petrol

Take care with the direction of the relationship. A piggyback contains coins. Of the options given, a car contains only petrol (or other fuel).

21 E gaze

The collective noun for rhinoceroses is crash or stubbornness. The collective noun for raccoons is gaze.

22 E eccentric

Eccentric, in relation to geometry, means circles that have centres that are not aligned. More generally it means unconventional or strange in views or behaviour.

23 B phase

Phase means a segment of time within a longer period, or to break up a long project into such distinct pieces which run one after another. Faze which means distract or disturb.

24 B born

Born means come into existence as an entity, either for a baby (or baby animal) or, figuratively, for an idea or organisation. Borne is a past tense of bear.

25 C patients

This is simply the plural of patient. There is no need for an apostrophe at all.

26 C pomposity

Pomposity is excessive pride and excessive feeling of self-importance; vanity or arrogance.

27 A deluded

Deluded means having a false, unshakeable belief. It implies that the person is suffering from a mental disorder. It is used figuratively to mean simply mistaken, but here its usage may be offensive.

28 D blissful

Blissful means very happy.

29 C defiance

Defiance is the act of defying someone or something. It fits well with an act of vandalism against a new authority figure.

30 E box

Box, in this sense, means to punch with a fist, or engage in a sporting contest involving this action.

Explanations for Training Session 28

1 E amusing

Hilarious means very funny. Synonyms are amusing, riotous, uproarious, hysterical, jolly, rollicking, lively.

2 E flamboyant

Florid means elaborate or intricate (and hinting that this may be excessively so). It also means a complexion that is flushed or reddened.

3 B misrepresent

To slander is to make a false statement about someone that damages their public reputation. Slander (noun) refers to that particular action, or the false statement itself.

4 E successful

Prosperous means successful in financial terms; having a high income and being considered a success.

5 A elaborate

Ornate means decorated to an extensive degree, and with great detail; elaborate or complex in design; lavish or ostentatious. The term can also be used figuratively to writing that is deliberately complex.

6 E favour

Incline means to be thinking favourably of doing or choosing something. It also means the habit of being inclined towards something: a preference or predilection. Incline also means a sloping surface.

7 B spiritual

Pious means strongly believing in religion and adhering to the requirements of that religion; devout, faithful, spiritual, righteous or reverent.

8 E agreeable

Contrary means in the opposite direction or nature. Of a person it indicates tending to disagree or refuse to go along with the group.

9 A morose

Jovial means friendly, cheery, good-humoured, genial, convivial, amiable, affable and sociable.

10 C irregular

Homogeneous (of a group of items, or a volume of fluid) means made up of identical parts; not showing differences between this and that or here and there.

11 C complain

An objective is the thing one wants to achieve: and aim or destination. Objective (adjective) means fair, neutral, dispassionate and unbiased.

12 C previous

All the other words mean having holes so that something (typically a liquid or air) can pass through. Previous means in the past.

13 A explosive

All the other words mean having an excessively high opinion of oneself and demanding respectful treatment from others.

14 C promise

All the other words can mean become smaller. Promise can mean the same as another meaning of contract, namely to agree on something formally. However in this question it is the odd one out.

15 B illusive

Elusive versus illusive. Elusive means difficult to find, understand or capture. Illusive means giving an illusory (false) appearance.

16 D inflict

All the other words refer to a pulling back from a position to an earlier position. Inflict means to cause something (especially harm) to happen to someone else.

17 B mollify

All the other words mean change. Mollify means reduce the level of anger or displeasure in a person.

18 'DDIE': the word is 'muddied'

Muddied means mixed up with mud, so that it is no longer transparent. There are two Ds together in the middle of the word, unlike studied.

19 B furtive

Those engaging in athletics are often sporty. Those engaging in thieving are often furtive. Derived from the Latin word "fur" for thief, it means trying to avoid attention in order to avoid punishment.

20 E nest

The structure in which bees live is called a hive; for hornets it is called a nest.

21 C game

Baseball is an example of a sport. Chess is an example of a game.

22 E disassemble

Disassemble is to separate into component parts. Do not confuse this with dissemble, which means to tell lies.

23 D solemnity

Solemnity means the degree to which someone or something is dignified and serious.

24 D likewise

Likewise means in a similar manner.

25 D abhorrent

Abhorrent means awful, terrible and disgusting. It has much more of an emotional component than aberrant, which merely indicates incorrect or outside the expected standard.

26 B sight

Sight is the noun related to seeing.

27 E countries'

They are the representatives of many countries, so write countries and add an apostrophe and an S

28 C turbid

Turbid refers to a liquid that might otherwise be clear but in fact is cloudy or murky because of small particles floating within it.

29 A noteworthy

Noteworthy means interesting or meaningful. All of the adjectives offered as options could fit grammatically, but noteworthy fits best with the mention of discussion being caused by the painting.

30 C practise

In British English, the verb is practise and the noun is practice. The two different words sound identical. The pattern is the same for advise (verb)/advice (noun) and license (verb)/licence (noun).

Explanations for Training Session 29

1 E idolize

Adore means either (of a person, creature or thing) love intensely, or (of a religious figure, concept or icon) worship, praise and venerate.

2 B recuperate

Recover means return to normal (after being weakened or injured) or find a possession (after losing it or having it stolen).

3 C reticent

Saying little.

4 A responsive

Receptive means willing to consider new ideas or willing to accept suggestions. In biology it also means able to detect signals.

5 B responsibility

A role is a responsibility or duty within a larger organisation; a job in a company or a part an actor plays in a film or play.

6 A resentment

Umbrage is annoyance or hostility as a reaction to something that has happened. It is commonly used in the phrase "took umbrage against".

7 E parallelism

An analogy is an explanation that points out how one thing or situation is similar to another, more familiar, one.

8 D assist

Restrain means hold back, control, limit freedom of action, or prevent someone from doing something. It can also refer to controlling oneself, preventing extreme emotion.

9 E ignore

To heed is to notice, and act on, information, a warning, guidance or advice. Heed (noun) is the attention that is paid to something.

10 D cancel

To provoke is to cause something to happen (initiate or instigate). It is often used more specifically to mean to annoy someone enough to trigger an (adverse) reaction.

11 C harmony

A malady is a disease or ailment. Figuratively it can be used to refer to a problem affecting a whole organisation or country, and which is difficult to solve.

12 E disrepair

All the other words mean the state in which others consider one to have done something bad. Disrepair is a state of not being repaired, such as an old building that has not been maintained.

13 A lesson

Lesson (a unit of teaching received) is different from lessen (reduce).

14 B lavish

All the other words mean obedient, bowing or fawning, including slavish means behaving like a slave. Lavish, in contrast, means using a large amount of resources and appearing luxurious or expensive.

15 D certain

All the other words indicate not being excited or excitable.

16 E ocean

All the other words mean a space or gap between other things. A gulf can (like ocean) mean a body of water, but the water must be specifically between two or more pieces of land, so still means a gap.

17 B extra

All the other words indicate a thing that has been chosen. Extra does not specifically mean chosen, rather it means additional. The term optional extra means an additional thing that has been chosen.

18 'CEIV': the word is 'conceive'

Conceive means imagine or give rise to a child. Like receive, it is an example of the rule that for the "EE" sound made up of an I and an E, it is I before E except after C.

19 E pack

The collective nouns for hounds is pack (the main term), but also cry, hunt, meet and stable.

20 A Italy

Noodles are a food made from rice flour, popular in Japan, China and other east Asian countries. A broadly similar dish made from wheat flour is spaghetti, characteristic of Italy and neighbouring countries.

21 C army

Army, colony, nest or swarm are collective nouns for ants.

22 E chauvinist

A chauvinist is a person with exaggerated or unreasonable preference for those of his or her own nationality. The term is also used for other forms of prejudice, such as between genders: a male chauvinist.

23 C climatic

Climatic means relating to a climate. Climactic means relating to the climax of something, such as a sporting event, film or speech.

24 D fanaticism

Fanaticism is the state of having intense enthusiasm and lack of critical thought about something; excessive zeal.

25 E crib

A crib sheet is a cheat sheet. It can also describe copying the work of another (especially in an exam) or, informally, a document to support study for an exam. It has a separate meaning of a cot for a baby.

26 E misspent

Misspent means spent in a poorly-chosen way (i.e. wastefully), most commonly in relation to money or time

27 C coarse

Coarse means unrefined, rough or harsh in texture; by extension it is also used to describe people who are rude, vulgar or in other ways unrefined.

28 B ascent

Ascent is the process of ascending (climbing up) something. Assent (noun) means approval for something, and the corresponding verb means to give such approval.

29 A experience

Experience is knowing about people and events from previous interactions. It can also refer to any occurrence which one learns from. Experience can also be a verb relating to these noun usages.

30 B certitude

Certitude is the intense and absolute certainty that something is true, in the mind of the person being described. It does not mean that the thing is actually true.

Explanations for Training Session 30

1 A essential

Integral means vital to make a thing complete; essential, necessary or basic. In mathematics it indicates a whole number, and in higher mathematics the calculation of an area under a curve.

2 A scold

To reproach is to criticise someone, typically for bad things that they have done. It particularly refers to telling them directly of one's disapproval.

3 E sorry

Contrite means genuinely sorry and apologetic for having done something wrong; remorseful, penitent, regretful, repentant, sheepish.

4 B queasy

Nauseous means feeling as though one is about to vomit. It can also mean the stimulus that is causing (or could cause) someone to be about to vomit.

5 B downcast

Sombre means low in spirit, downcast, dejected, sad, depressed, despondent, or dispirited.

6 C slaughter

To sacrifice means to give up a possession with the aim of gaining something of greater importance. It also has a specific meaning of killing a person or creature to gain favour with God or gods.

7 C accepting

To be resigned is to have accepted something unpleasant because one has no choice. Separately, to resign is to voluntarily give up a job. (That someone resigns does not mean that they are replaced.)

8 C start

Conclusion means the end of something. Conclusion can also mean the final judgement on something, arrived at by a process of reasoning. In this question, start (noun) is the antonym.

9 E dull

Compelling means overwhelmingly persuasive or very interesting. Synonyms are convincing, cogent, forceful, credible, sound, rational, irrefutable; or (for the second meaning) gripping, fascinating, riveting.

10 A initiate

To simulate is to create the appearance of something else, either for deception, practice, entertainment. Simulate also indicates creating the appearance of an emotion, or creating a mathematical model.

11 A separation

Distress means sorry, pain or severe anxiety. Synonyms are heartbreak, discomfort, torment, ache, pain, anguish, heartache. A person in distress is in need (of help).

12 B adjective

All the words mean in excess of requirements, except adjective which is a class of words.

13 E uniform

All the other words mean based on something that is not solid, and therefore may not be correct, may not last, or may collapse.

14 D sentimental

All the other words mean talking a great deal.

15 E confidant

Confident versus confidant. All the other words mean confident and lacking doubt. A confidant is a person whom one trusts to tell secrets.

16 D flicker

All the other words mean grow well or be successful.

17 B bazaar

All the other words mean strange or unusual. A bazaar is a market, particularly in the Middle East.

18 'UARA': the word is 'guarantee'

Guarantee means promise of good performance, backed by a promise to replace the item or refund the cost. It may help to think of the first four letters as the beginning of "guard".

19 B ostentation

For peacocks, the collective nouns are ostentation, pride and muster. These derive from the showy appearance of the displayed feathers. Muster, in military terms, means assemble troops for inspection.

20 C coin

The commonest outline shape of a painting is a rectangle. Likewise the commonest outline shape of a coin is a circle.

21 C troop

The collective noun for baboons is troop.

22 D Curious

She may have been clueless, but curious fits the rest of the sentence better because curiosity would be a stronger driver to look in a place than ignorance would.

23 D deserted

Desert means a waterless land. Desert (verb) means to abandon a person. It can be used figuratively for a skill that becomes suddenly unavailable. Dessert is a light dish served after the main meal.

24 A aspect

Aspect means a feature or view. It would be possible to be unhappy with one room (out of many booked, e.g. for a large family) but "which room of it" would not be a natural way to phrase that question.

25 E years'

It is the work of two years, and so should be written years'. Tip: If this is difficult to remember, imagine it was the work of two teachers (not two years): how would you write it? Two teachers' work.

26 B circumstance

A circumstance is the background of an event. Most often used in the plural, circumstances are facts or conditions which impact on an event. Circumstances are also a euphemism for financial status.

27 E denote

Connote is to imply in a gentle way, whereas denote is to define exactly. For example, "half" denotes 50%, whereas "many" connotes perhaps over 50% is not perfectly clear on the matter.

28 E loose

Loose versus lose. Loose means free, untied, unbound, unrestricted. It can also mean badly behaved and unruly. Lose means to misplace or be deprived of something.

29 B nemesis

Nemesis means a deserved punishment that eventually arrives and cannot be escaped. The word comes from the ancient Greek goddess of retribution.

30 A its

Its is a possessive PRONOUN, an exception to the rule that possessives have an apostrophe. Tip: Can the word be rewritten "it is"? If so, the spelling is "it's". Otherwise write "its", just like "his".

Explanations for Training Session 31

1 D ancestor

Forebear versus forbear. ForEbear means ancestor: one who has lived beforE. Forbear (without the first E) means give up, sacrifice, something or some habit.

2 A abandon

To forsake is to leave someone or abandon them, when one would be expected to have a continuing duty to care for them. It also means give up a habit that one enjoyed.

3 A dependable

Steadfast means faithful, devoted, dedicated, dependable or reliable. It is applied to people to remain over a long time loyal to certain people or principles of behaviour.

4 D stare

To contemplate is to consider something for a long time. The term implies deep analysis. It is used most often for looking at an object or considering a thought.

5 C awkward

Stubborn means sticking to one point of view despite pressure to change it. It implies that the person is wrong or is being unreasonable. Of a stain or disease, stubborn indicates difficult to remove or cure.

6 C preserve

Retain means keep ownership or possession of something, or protect it during a process of change, or (of a thought or fact) remember it.

7 C beautiful

Aesthetic means relating to beautiful appearance, or the process of achieving beauty or appreciating it. It is more often applied to a painting, sculpture or building than to a person.

8 E subtle

Obvious means easily understood or noticed; self-evident, plain, clear, striking, prominent, noticeable, perceptible, visible.

9 D flimsy

Sturdy means strong and solid. It may refer to a person whose build is solid or muscular, or a thing which is designed to be strong.

10 C altitude

Hostile means unfriendly or having hatred; confrontational, bellicose or belligerent; pugnacious, antagonistic, truculent, combative.

11 D poetry

Adversary means enemy, competitor or opponent.

12 B underground

All the other words indicate work done to a high standard where even minor features are attended to.

13 D suing

All the other words mean subsequent, including ensuing. Suing means taking legal action against.

14 B overwork

All the other words mean constrain or limit.

15 D cower

All the other words mean someone who has stopped being loyal during a conflict, and has changed sides.

16 C perturbed

All the other words mean showing gentleness, compassion and tenderness. Perturbed means upset or disturbed.

17 D impulse

All the other words mean quick or rapid. Impulse is a noun meaning a sudden feeling of wanting to do something, or a push to do something.

18 'SCIE': the word is 'conscience'

Conscience means the judgement of what is right and wrong, that supervises our choice of behaviour. To spell it, it may help to note that the second part is simply "science": just add "con" at the left.

19 A company

The collective noun for moles is company, labour or (rarely) movement.

20 B throw

The important act on a football during a game is that the players kick it. The corresponding important act on a javelin (a spear-like projectile) is for the athlete to throw it.

21 D flight

Flight is the collective noun for butterflies, birds, doves and swallows, as well as (arguably) for cormorants and goshawks.

22 C pose

They paint 1/12 and 1/6 of a hall per day, respectively. Together, 1/12+1/6 =1/12+2/12=3/12=1/4 of a hall per day. The Eureka! Challenging Maths workbooks give tips and tricks for such tricky questions.

23 D paradox

A paradox is a statement that at first seems wrong, contradictory or nonsensical, but when investigated carefully turns out to be correct. Baffling and unexplained do not fit grammatically because of the "a".

24 B including

Including VAT (or anything else) means the cost of the VAT has already been calculated as part of the number being shown.

25 A insure

To insure is to pay regularly now, in order in future to receive compensation if there is damage or loss of property, or injury or death of a person. This is different from ensure, to make something certain.

26 E resplendent

Resplendent means dazzlingly attractive and impressive because of the degree of colour or luxury.

27 E aviary

The best word to complete the sentence is aviary, a large enclosure for birds that allows them considerable freedom to fly.

28 C foliage

Foliage is leaves of plants, especially trees, considered together a single large group. There are no villagers: it was uninhabited. One protester (or one leaf) would not have been able to block every step.

29 E inconspicuous

Inconspicuous means not attracting attention; unnoticeable, unremarkable, unexceptional, modest, discreet. A more extreme form would be hidden or concealed.

30 D auspicious

Auspicious means indicating success or an indication of good chances of future success.

Explanations for Training Session 32

1 E unwarranted

Gratuitous means done in excess of what is necessary or appropriate. In particular this word is used for violence that is not necessary, for example, violence done in addition to a robbery.

2 A trigger

To precipitate is to cause something to begin suddenly, particularly when the thing is unpleasant; trigger, spark, provoke, instigate. It also means to rain. Precipitate (adjective) means reckless or unwise.

3 E hiatus

A respite is a pause in something that is otherwise prolonged, continuous and unpleasant, such as a siege, pain, or heavy responsibility.

4 A genuine

Authentic means genuinely what it is stated to be; real, truthful, honest. Antonyms are counterfeit, fake, phoney.

5 B nauseated

Bilious can mean suffering from nausea (a feeling of being about to vomit), or grumpy, ill-tempered and easily angered.

6 D confuse

Bemuse versus amuse. To bemuse means to confuse or make bewildered. To amuse is to entertain or to cause to laugh by being funny.

7 D reply

To respond is to reply or give an answer. This can be in speech, in writing (via a letter or email) or through an action.

8 D perfected

Marred means spoilt, damaged, impaired or worsened. The word is commonly used when something is generally good except for one aspect which spoils it.

9 C receive

To transmit is to make something (often information) move from one place to another or many places (such as in a television, radio or internet broadcast).

10 A cultivated

To foster is to encourage something to develop, or to take care of a child who was originally born to other parents. Cultivate would be synonym, but cultivateD (adjective) means sophisticated or educated.

11 E fertiliser

To mature is to grow up or move from infant form to adult form.

12 A surplus

All the other words mean make it possible for something to continue by providing support. Surplus means in excess of requirements.

13 C succumb

All the other words mean contend or wrestle with, and can be applied to an opponent or a problem in general. Succumb means to lose in such a contest or to die after battling a disease.

14 E different

All the other words mean shy or reluctant to be the centre of attention; demure, retiring.

15 A avocado

All the other words mean someone who supports a thing, a person or an idea. An avocado is a fruit.

16 C tented

All the other words mean watchful or keeping a close eye on something. Tented means lifted up in the middle, like the cloth of a tent once it has been set up.

17 C reticent

Reluctant versus reticent. Reluctant means unwilling to do something. Reticent means quiet and uncommunicative. A reticent person may be reluctant to speak, but the words are different.

18 'HIE': the word is 'chief'

I before E. Incidentally, it is fortunate that the word was not chef, the French word from which the word chief is derived. Finding oneself delivered to the chef would be a rather worse situation.

19 A pride

The widely recognised collective noun for lions is the pride. A less well known term is sawt.

20 D six

A square has four-fold symmetry. A snowflake has six-fold symmetry.

21 E murder

Murder is the collective noun for crows or magpies. In the 15th century, their dark colour and eyes made crows seem messengers of the devil. A crow landing on a house signalled that someone inside would die.

22 A taciturn

Taciturn means quiet, reserved and uncommunicative; untalkative, reticent, unforthcoming, mute, shy, unresponsive, inarticulate.

23 A elliptical

Elliptical means shaped like an ellipse, i.e. oval. Unrelatedly, it means tending to omit parts, words or letters, which cn mk thngs dfclt to undrstnd!

24 C homonym

Homonyms are two or more words that have the same spelling and/or same pronunciation, but different meanings.

25 D veto

Veto is the right of certain individuals or organisations to block a law or decision made by a lower authority. Veto (verb) means to block through this power.

26 D ostensibly

Ostensibly means apparently or based on outward appearances. It implies that this appearance does not reflect the truth.

27 C repast

Repast means a meal, feast or banquet. It implies the meal is large and the food is plentiful.

28 B rapture

Rapture means extreme happiness or bliss. It is used in religious contexts and also figuratively to indicate great happiness with something or with events.

29 D surly

Surly means unfriendly and ill-tempered. Synonyms are grumpy, prickly, irascible (easily angered), short-tempered, cantankerous, crabby, sullen and sulky.

30 B taut

Taut means stretched tightly, pulled with tension, tense. It can be applied to a film or writing to indicate that it is concise and perhaps exciting.

Explanations for Training Session 33

1 C objective

Purpose means the objective for which one is aiming, or the reason that a thing is needed. Purpose also means the appearance of being determined.

2 A greedy

Avaricious means greedy for money; rapacious, covetous, grasping, mercenary, materialistic.

3 E praise

Exalt versus exult. To exAlt is to glorify, for example in a religious ceremony. To exUlt is to rejoice, for example when one hears good news.

4 D apprehension

Trepidation is the feeling that something bad is about to happen; fear, anxiety, dread, apprehension, worry, tension, unease, foreboding, alarm.

5 B striking

Singular means (in grammar) relating to just one rather than many. Used more generally, it means outstanding, excellent, striking, remarkable; it subtly hints at one of a kind rather than one of many.

6 B debate

Controversy means a long-lasting state of dispute in a public environment, with two or more conflicting viewpoints being put forward by various participants.

7 B order

Prescribe versus proscribe. Prescribe means recommend or order, for example a doctor advising on what medication to take. In contrast, proscribe means officially forbid or ban.

8 A infuriating

To pacify is to make someone less angry; placate, appease, quieten, calm, soothe, mollify.

9 E lenience

Austerity (of a person) means lacking in kindness, lenience or friendliness; severe, stern, harsh, unforgiving. Austerity also means a time of reduced spending because of shortage of money in a country.

10 D calculate

An action is a thing that is done, i.e. An operation, movement or deed. A measure (noun) taken can be an action that is done.

11 C organisation

A partner is someone with whom one works towards a common goal; teammate, associate, co-worker, collaborator, ally, comrade. It also means boyfriend, girlfriend, husband or wife.

12 E gripping

All the other words mean having a strong focus on obtaining money. Grasping and gripping do share a meaning but gripping has no meaning in common with the others.

13 E sauce

All the other words mean the person or organisation from which something first comes. Sauce is unrelated and only sounds like source.

14 A ocean

All the other words (including divine) mean to predict the future in some way.

15 D corroborate

All the other words mean come together or work together. Corroborate means confirm, in the sense that a second piece of information confirms a first piece of information as correct.

16 A offer

All the other words mean occur or happen, including befall which is rather old-fashioned. Offer is unrelated.

17 C internal

All the other words mean intense, strong, and powerful. Internal means inside.

18 'ICIE': the word is 'efficiency'

Efficiency is the habit or achievement of delivering a large effect for the amount of resources consumed. When the main resource is time, efficiency is speed.

19 C swarm

The collective noun for caterpillar is army. Insects as a whole have many collective nouns, but swarm is the most widely applicable.

20 C pan

One bakes in an oven, but one fries in a pan or in oil. Of these two, pan resembles an oven better (albeit still imperfectly) since it is a permanent device and not discarded at each cooking session.

21 B parliament

For owls and rooks, the collective term is parliament.

22 B lose

Loose versus lose. Loose means free, untied, unbound, unrestricted. It can also mean badly behaved and unruly. Lose means to misplace or be deprived of something.

23 A castigate

Castigate means severely reprimand; admonish, rebuke, chastise, chide, upbraid, berate, lambast.

24 C assiduous

Assiduous means showing great care and perseverance.

25 B lampoon

Lampoon means to publically criticise someone, making them look foolish, using ridicule, irony or sarcasm.

26 C opulent

Opulent means luxuriously decorated in a manner that seems expensive, extravagant or excessive. One might be horrified at the extravagance but this does not appear to be the feeling of the writer.

27 E concede

To concede means to acknowledge or admit that one has been defeated.

28 E collage

Collage is a style of artistic creation which uses pieces of coloured paper or pieces of other pictures to make a new picture. It is French for "sticking".

29 C milliner

A milliner is a maker, fitter, or seller, of hats for women.

30 B scintillating

Scintillating, in ordinary use, means very clever, interesting and amusing. In science it means sparkling or producing many small points of light.

Explanations for Training Session 34

1 C solemn

Staid, of a person, indicates serious, respectable, unexciting, unadventurous, steady and conventional.

2 B renounce

Forebear versus forbear. ForEbear means ancestor: one who has lived beforE. Forbear (without the first E) means give up, sacrifice, something or some habit.

3 C scruples

Conscience versus conscious. Conscience (or scruples) is the human judgement that distinguishes right from wrong. Conscious means knowing, being awake, or being aware.

4 D form

Structure means a building or other object made according to a plan, or the relation of the various parts within the overall whole. Structure (verb) means to make an organisation or agreement.

5 D assembly

A convention is a formal assembly of people representing many others. Separately, convention means an agreement (either formally documented or by informal general agreement) on how things should be done.

6 E disproves

To belie something means to show it to be false; contradict, undermine, debunk, refute, disprove

7 E undertaking

A project is a plan or scheme, especially if it is major, involving many people or a lot of time. Project (verb) means throw, or predict for the future, or display an image.

8 C unassuming

Imperious means having a tendency to order people around; authoritarian, dictatorial, domineering, overbearing.

9 E release

Seize means take under one's control by grabbing it physically or using legal or military steps. Figuratively it is used to mean to grab an idea and act on it.

10 B definable

Agreeable (of a place or experience) means enjoyable and pleasant; nice, appealing, satisfying, charming, delightful. Agreeable (of a person) means willing to agree to something.

11 E suspicious

Prolific means producing a great deal of writing, music, flowers or ideas.

12 B dialogue

All the other words mean a document which stores information about what happened. Synonyms annals, list, roll, roster.

13 E drizzling

All the other words mean difficult or advanced within a field of knowledge. Drizzling means raining lightly.

14 D ripcord

All the other words mean conflict or disagreement. A ripcord is a piece of string or rope that is pulled to activate a mechanism, particularly opening a parachute.

15 B company

All the other words mean having a limit, a maximum or a restriction. Company is an unrelated word, even though some companies are limited.

16 B gamble

All the other words mean give support or help to someone or something, including abet. It is not related to a bet, and therefore gamble is the odd one out.

17 D inflammable

Inflammable (and flammable) versus inflammatory. Confusingly inflammABLE and flammABLE mean the same, which is easily set on fire. InflammATORY means causing (or intended to cause) angry feelings.

18 'CEIT': the word is 'deceitful'

Deceitfulness is the habit or tendency to give false or misleading information to gain advantage. For the EE sound consisting of an I and an E, it is I before E except after C, as in this case.

19 D team

While team is the principal collective noun for horses that are in harness (e.g. pulling a plough), less specific collective nouns for horses include band, string, herd, stable and haras (also spelt harrase).

20 B pours

One sucks on a straw, and scoops or pours with a ladle. One can scoop (and perhaps spoon) with a ladle but, without an S at the end, they do not fit.

21 D flock

A general collective noun for ducks is flock, but there are additional ones for specific situations, such as bunch, paddling and raft for ducks on water, and skein, string and team for ducks in flight.

22 A relegate

Relegate means demote, or move to a group of lower status or rank. For example, a sports team that loses frequently may be relegated to a lower league.

23 A assailant

Assailant means attacker: the person who assaults someone else.

24 C goad

To goad is to continually annoy or irritate a person or group until a reaction is obtained. As a noun, it means a stick for poking cattle.

25 B monotonous

Monotonous means dull or repetitive; literally with a single tone throughout. Delivery is the way the words are said, and can be exciting.

26 D odious

Odious means hateful or extremely unpleasant. It has a special meaning in international relations, of debt incurred by a country by illegitimate or extremely unjust leaders.

27 E onerous

Onerous is an adjective indicating that a task, responsibility or duty involves great labour, mental effort or worry.

28 C garrulous

Garrulous means excessively talkative. Synonyms are loquacious, voluble, verbose, chatty, effusive, jabbering.

29 A sumptuous

Sumptuous means impressive, lavish, magnificent, extravagant and expensive in appearance. Synonyms: grand, lush, palatial, opulent, deluxe.

30 A terminate

End.

The Non-Verbal Ninja

Intensive Training through *Visual* Explanations

Comprehensive course from basics to advanced puzzles
Answers and explanations given graphically
3-volume set systematically tackling the numerous CEM puzzle types
600 questions designed to build efficient strategies for success

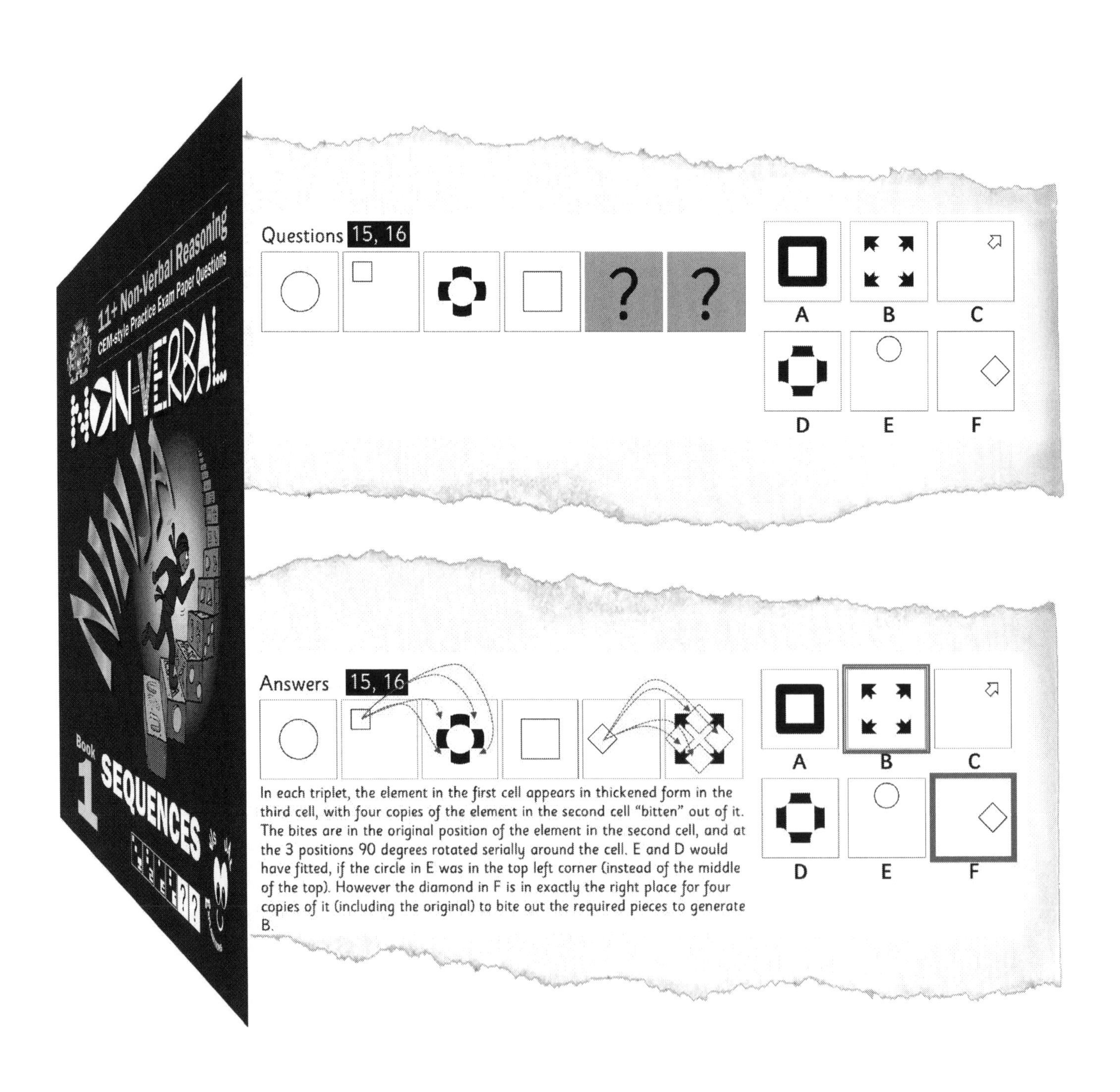

Questions **29, 30**

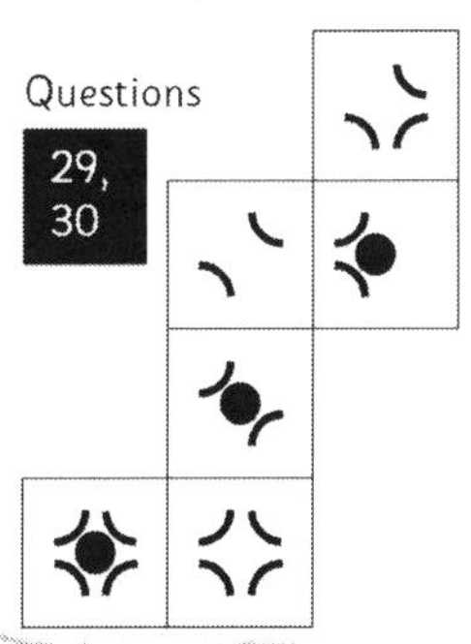

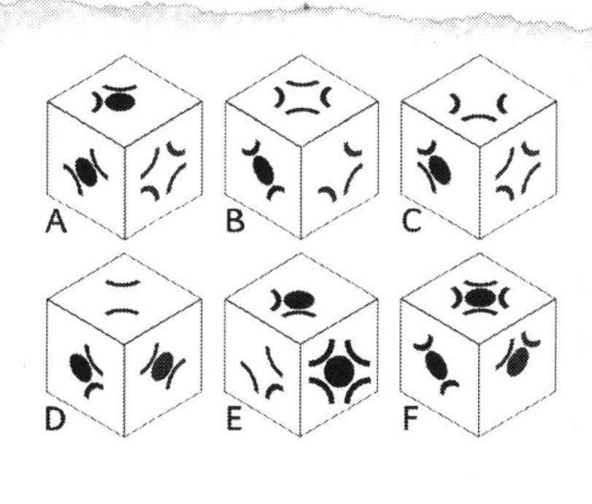

Answers **29, 30**

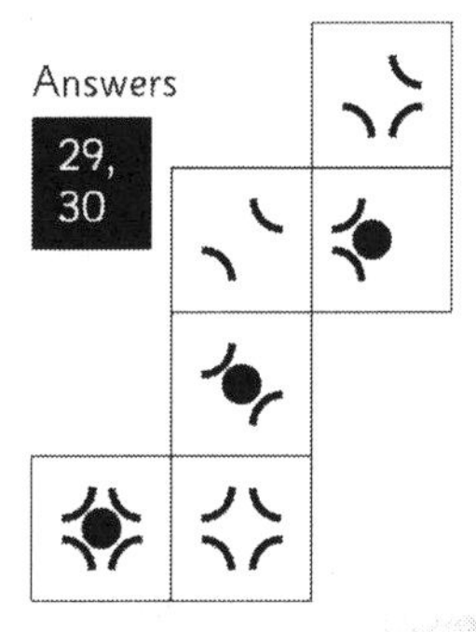

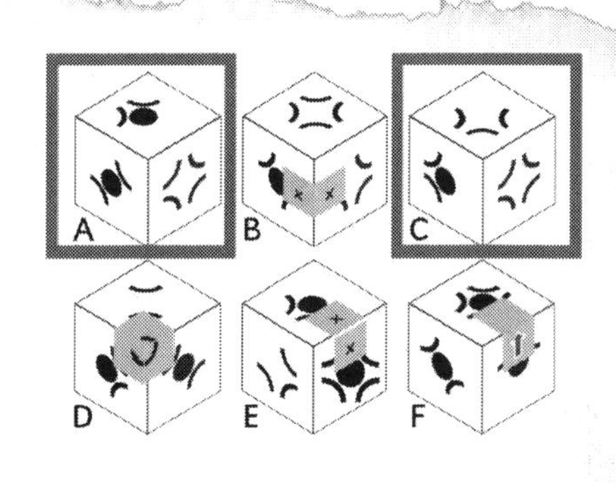

Question **13**

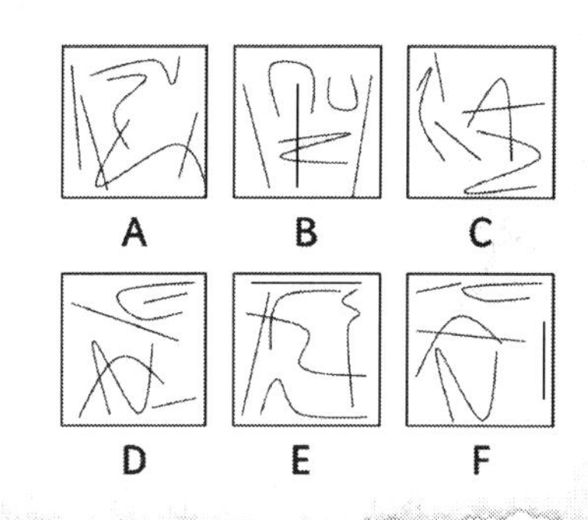

Answer **13**

Each cell has three straight lines and three curved lines. In the top row, all crossings are between two straight lines. In the bottom row, all crossings are between two curved lines.

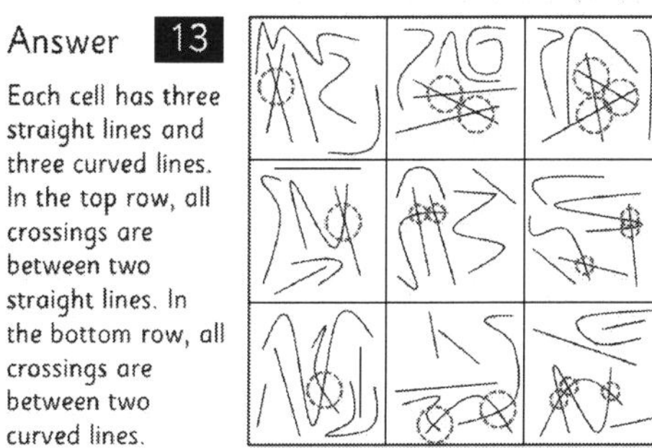

In the middle row, all crossings are between a curved and a straight line. In the left column, there is 1 crossing. In the middle, there are 2. In the right column, there are 3.

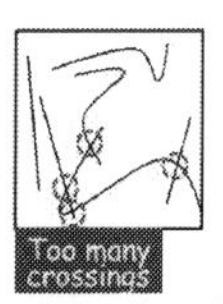

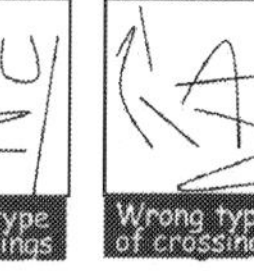

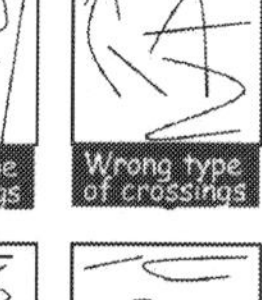

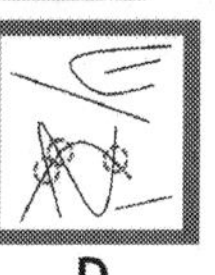

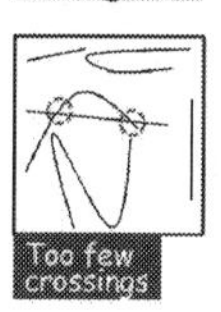

Printed in Great Britain
by Amazon